Caught Up

A STUDY ON 1 & 2 THESSALONIANS

STACY DAVIS & BRENDA HARRIS

EDITORIAL TEAM

PASTOR CHRIS SWANSEN
Theological Editor,
Calvary Chapel Chester Springs

PASTOR STEVEN DORR
Pastoral Support,
Calvary Chapel Chester Springs

CARINNA LAROCCO
Copy Editor

JOAN PURDY
Copy and Content Editor

MELISSA BEREDA
Graphic Designer

LYNN JENSEN
Office Support

CARINA DANIELLE
Photographer

CHRIS GOOD
Media Support

JANET GOOD
DANIELLE ROSSNEY
Video Support

CAUGHT UP
A Study on the Books of 1 & 2 Thessalonians
Part of the Delighting in the Lord Bible Study Series

© Copyright 2023
Calvary Chapel Chester Springs
PO Box 595, Eagle, PA 19480

All rights reserved. No part of this book may be reproduced or transmitted in any form or by any means, electronic or mechanical, including photocopying and recording, or by any information storage or retrieval system, except as may be expressly permitted in writing by the publisher.

ISBN 9798853227668

Unless otherwise indicated, Scripture quotations are from the New King James Version of the Bible.
Copyright © 1982 by Thomas Nelson, Inc. Used by permission.
All rights reserved.

Ministry verse Psalm 27:4 is taken from the Holy Bible, New Living Translation (NLT), copyright © 1996, 2004, 2015 by Tyndale House Foundation. Used by permission of Tyndale House Publishers, Inc., Carol Stream, Illinois 60188.
All rights reserved.

Scripture taken from the HOLY BIBLE, NEW INTERNATIONAL VERSION ®. Copyright © 1973, 1978, 1984 by International Bible Society. Used by permission of Zondervan.
All rights reserved.

Scripture quotations taken from the (NASB®) New American Standard Bible®, Copyright© 1960, 1971, 1977, 1995, 2020 by The Lockman Foundation. Used by permission, All rights reserved. lockman.org

Cover Design: Melissa Bereda
Cover Photo: Shutterstock: Wirestock Creators
Cloud Photos: Elise Bereda

TABLE OF CONTENTS

4	MEET THE AUTHORS	
6-7	OUR APPROACH: R.E.A.D. THE BIBLE	
8	STUDY SUGGESTIONS	
9	HOW TO USE THIS STUDY	
10	DELIGHTING IN MY SALVATION	
11-20	WEEK 1	Introduction to 1 & 2 Thessalonians
21-34	WEEK 2	Caught Up in the Gospel: 1 Thessalonians 1 Teaching Notes
35-48	WEEK 3	Caught Up in Pleasing God: 1 Thessalonians 2 Teaching Notes
49-64	WEEK 4	Caught Up in a Faith-Filled Life: 1 Thessalonians 3 Teaching Notes
65-82	WEEK 5	Caught Up with an Eternal Perspective: 1 Thessalonians 4 Teaching Notes
83-100	WEEK 6	Caught Up in God's Will: 1 Thessalonians 5 Teaching Notes
101-116	WEEK 7	Don't Get Caught Up in Your Circumstances: 2 Thessalonians 1 Teaching Notes
117-132	WEEK 8	Don't Get Caught Up in Fear and Worry: 2 Thessalonians 2 Teaching Notes
133-150	WEEK 9	Don't Get Caught Up in Distractions: 2 Thessalonians 3 Teaching Notes
151-152	SCRIPTURE MEMORY CARDS	
153	WORKS CITED	
154-157	OTHER DELIGHTING IN THE LORD STUDIES	

MEET THE AUTHORS

Stacy Davis

Stacy Davis has been teaching women God's Word for over 15 years. She has learned many biblical truths through difficult trials. Beginning at the age of three with her mother's brain aneurysm, to the death of her fourth son, and through invasive breast cancer, Stacy's faith has been tried and tested many times over. Her life gives testimony to God's redeeming and transforming power. Stacy teaches with passion the truths of God's Word desiring women to experience Christ's love and victory in their lives. She lives in Pennsylvania with her husband, Barclay. They have five adult children, three daughters-in-love, and a son waiting for them in heaven.

Stacy@delightinginthelord.com

Brenda Harris

Brenda Harris' background in education was foundational to the plans God had for her to serve Him. In 2006, she transitioned away from instructing young people how to read literature and began teaching women how they can have a closer walk with the Lord through reading and studying their Bible. From a young age, dyslexia both defined and affected Brenda's life. God has shown her what the world views as a weakness, God uses as a strength. She is an enthusiastic teacher who loves a great visual to help demonstrate practical ways to apply God's Word to real life. Brenda lives in Pennsylvania with her husband, Michael. They have two adult children.

Brenda@delightinginthelord.com

"FOR THE LORD HIMSELF
WILL DESCEND FROM HEAVEN WITH A SHOUT,
WITH THE VOICE OF AN ARCHANGEL,
AND WITH THE TRUMPET OF GOD.
AND THE DEAD IN CHRIST WILL RISE FIRST.
THEN WE WHO ARE ALIVE AND REMAIN SHALL BE
CAUGHT UP
TOGETHER WITH THEM IN THE CLOUDS
TO MEET THE LORD IN THE AIR.
AND THUS WE SHALL ALWAYS BE WITH THE LORD.
THEREFORE COMFORT ONE ANOTHER
WITH THESE WORDS."

1 THESSALONIANS 4:16-18

OUR APPROACH TO GOD'S WORD

To get the most out of this study, you will want to ensure the time spent studying God's Word is not just an academic exercise but is for your personal application and life transformation. The goal of studying God's Word is to know God; who He is, what He has done, and why this is important for you. Studying the Bible should increase your faith in God. As you read the Bible, God is interacting with you. Your study time becomes a life-giving, life-changing experience, not just head knowledge. However, God's Word can only be personal and life-changing when the Spirit of the Living God is in your heart (John 14:17).

As soon as this spiritual transformation takes place in your heart, the Holy Spirit communicates with your spirit all the truths found in God and made known through Jesus Christ.

Jesus is the only way to be born of the Spirit and to have eternal life. This is how the study of God's Word becomes personal. It begins with a personal relationship through faith in Jesus Christ. If you've never accepted Jesus as your Lord and Savior, turn to the Delighting in My Salvation page of this study. This is your first step.

THE R.E.A.D. APPROACH

All the Delighting in the Lord studies use a study model we developed called R.E.A.D. This model takes you through reading the verses, experiencing and understanding the details of the verses, applying them to your life, and finishing with delighting in what you have learned about God. The DITL studies are all verse-by-verse in their approach, allowing Scripture to interpret Scripture as you study. Our hope in writing these studies is that you will learn to understand the Bible and the heart of God.

Each week of study takes you through the R.E.A.D. approach. The week begins with an introduction that leads you into the content of the Scripture about to be studied.

OPEN IN PRAYER

Luke 24:45 tells us, "He [Jesus] opened their understanding, that they might comprehend the Scriptures." After Jesus rose from the dead, He appeared before His disciples on numerous occasions. He spoke these words to them shortly before ascending into heaven. Jesus helped them understand the Scriptures; all that had been written in the Law of Moses, the Prophets, and the Psalms to that point.

It is the same for us. Jesus will open our understanding to the Bible.

For this reason, we encourage you to start in prayer every time you approach God's Word. Ask God to open your mind to His understanding, to make His Word clear to you, and to reveal truths of who He is.

Receiving God's Word

With each week of study, start by reading the designated verses from beginning to end. This will help you understand the big picture of what is being said as well as see the context. You may see consistencies, repeated words, and themes being developed. Read slowly and thoughtfully.

Experiencing God's Word

The Experiencing portion is where you will interact with God through His Word to gain spiritual understanding. In this section you will go verse-by-verse answering inductive and deductive questions. You will observe details, see connections, and interpret what is being said within context so that you can draw conclusions. There might also be questions that have you looking in other books of the Bible.

Each week's verses are broken into smaller experience sections designated by Experience 1, 2, and 3. An estimated time frame is given for each section. Experience 1 will cover the whole chapter for the week asking general observation questions given in the text. Experience 2 and 3 of each week will explore themes presented in the verses in more detail.

Acting on God's Word

In this part of the study, you will be applying the verses to your life. Hebrews 4:12 says, "For the word of God is living and powerful, and sharper than any two-edged sword, piercing even to the division of soul and spirit, and of joints and marrow, and is a discerner of the thoughts and intents of the heart." Through the Holy Spirit, God's Word will speak to the deep places of your life.

In this section we ask questions examining personal application from the biblical principles presented in the week's lesson.

Delighting in God's Word

Our ministry's foundational verse is Psalm 27:4. This verse tells us to delight in the Lord's perfections and to meditate in His temple. In this final section, you will end by writing a verse from the chapter you just finished studying. This verse is also on a scripture memory card at the back of the book. We encourage you to memorize each weekly verse.

STUDY SUGGESTIONS

COMMITMENT AND PLANNING
Dedication and a time commitment will be needed to get the full benefit of this study. Plan on setting aside 1–2 hours a week to complete the whole week's study. You will find that your investment in God's Word will be seen in your spiritual growth. Plan on coming to study with your weekly lesson completed.

BIBLE TRANSLATIONS
The DITL studies use the New King James version (NKJV) of the Bible when writing the study questions. You may find it easier to use this same translation. We recommend using a literal Bible translation such as KJV, NASB or ESV for the study if you don't use the NKJV.

BIBLE COMMENTARIES AND RESOURCES
We recommend that you don't use any Bible commentaries or resources until after you have studied the weekly verses yourself, allowing the Holy Spirit to direct your understanding. It can be tempting to read the commentary in study Bibles and online. Give yourself time to understand what is being said in each verse before turning to resources. We promise you that God will give you light bulb moments in your study time as you dig into the verses yourself. If you find yourself struggling with a question, leave the answer blank and bring that question to your small group discussion time.

In the study you may notice references to Strong's Concordance. It may look something like this: *Firstborn* is *protokos* (Strong's G4416). When you see this, it means that we are giving you the original word used in either the Hebrew (Old Testament) or Greek (New Testament) so that you can better understand the word usage. This often helps give a deeper understanding of what is being said through the use of that word.

HERE ARE SOME SUGGESTED RESOURCES TO USE AFTER YOU'VE COMPLETED EACH WEEK'S QUESTIONS:

- *The Bible Knowledge Commentary* by Walvoord and Zook
- Warren Wiersbe Commentaries
- www.blueletterbible.org
- *The New Strong's Exhaustive Concordance of the Bible*
- *Vine's Complete Expository Dictionary of Old and New Testament Words*

HOW TO USE THIS STUDY

INDIVIDUAL OR SMALL GROUP
The DITL studies can be used individually or with a group. If using on your own, we suggest doing the study pages over the course of a week. If you are doing the study with a group, we recommend all ladies complete the study on their own throughout the week. When the ladies meet, break a large group into smaller ones; each group with a leader to guide the discussion of the week's lesson. Be sure to incorporate prayer into your study time.

TEACHING VIDEOS
A teaching video accompanies each week of the study, except for the introduction week. There are pages for taking notes provided in the workbook for all the other weeks. The videos are a supplement to the study and not required. The study is written to guide you deep into the verses yourself. Our goal is for you to gain a personal understanding of the verses and books being studied as you are guided by the Holy Spirit and learn on your own. Should you desire the teaching component of the study, our videos can be viewed on the ministry website: www.delightinginthelord.com. A free teaching video set can also be requested for groups by emailing info@delightinginthelord.com.

WEEK 1 FORMAT:
The first week of study introduces you to the books of 1 and 2 Thessalonians. It will cover the biblical authors, as well as the overall context of the letters. If you are leading a group, we recommend going through the lesson together on the first week of Bible study for the ladies to get acquainted with the format and content. It can serve as an example of what they can expect to do weekly at home. Week 1 will give background on 1 and 2 Thessalonians while also asking questions. The questions will help give you an understanding of why the book was written, to whom, by whom, and events surrounding the writing, so you understand the biblical and historical context.

If you are leading a discussion group and have any questions about the study, please reach out to Brenda and Stacy at info@delightinginthelord.com.

LET'S GET STARTED!
We are so thrilled that you have chosen to study God's Word. There is truly nothing better you can be doing with your time. The benefit will overflow into all areas of your life as God works through you by the power of His Word. We are praying for you.

In Christ's love,

Brenda and Stacy

DELIGHTING IN MY SALVATION

God desires a personal relationship with you. Maybe you've never heard that before. He loves you so much that He sent His Son, Jesus, to die on the cross for you. In His love for you, God provided His Son, Jesus Christ, to be the perfect sacrifice for your sin. When Jesus was crucified on the cross nearly 2,000 years ago, God put the sins of the whole world onto His perfect Son, Jesus, so that through Him you'd have forgiveness and eternal life. Jesus paid the penalty for your sin and provided a way to God.

The first step in receiving the forgiveness Jesus offers is by acknowledging you have lived your life apart from Him. You have followed your own motives and desires. In God's eyes, this is sin. Sin carries eternal consequences and separation from God. Salvation begins with repentance. Everyone must recognize they are sinful human beings in need of a Savior. Jesus is the answer to our sin problem. If you have never prayed to Jesus to ask Him into your heart, it is a simple prayer of acknowledging your faith in Jesus and asking Him to forgive you of your sins.

THE CONVERSATION WITH GOD IS LIKE THIS...

"Dear God, I admit I am a sinner and have lived my life doing what I want. You are perfectly holy, and I am not. My sin grieves You and separates me from You. Please forgive me."

"For all have sinned and fall short of the glory of God." (Romans 3:23)

"I believe that You provided Jesus Christ as the answer for my sin through His death on the cross. He paid my sin debt in full. He is my perfect substitute. Because of Him, I am cleansed forever from my sin."

"For the wages of sin is death, but the gift of God is eternal life in Christ Jesus our Lord." (Romans 6:23)

"Lord, please come into my heart and life. From this day forward, I desire to know You more and want to begin a personal relationship with You as my Savior and Lord. Thank You for Your free gift of salvation and that I am no longer separated from You but am filled with You by the power of the Holy Spirit."

"If you confess with your mouth the Lord Jesus and believe in your heart that God has raised Him from the dead, you will be saved." (Romans 10:9)

"Thank You, God, for forgiving me. Please help me to grow to know You better and to live a life that pleases You from this day forward. Amen."

If you have prayed to accept Christ as your Savior, please tell someone today!
Share this exciting news with a close Christian friend, your small group leader, or your pastor.
They will be thrilled to encourage you in your faith and your decision to follow Jesus!

WEEK 1

INTRODUCTION TO 1 & 2 THESSALONIANS

Whether this is your first Bible study or one of many done over the years, it's likely you've heard about the Apostle Paul. Of the 27 books in the New Testament, Paul wrote 13 of them. Each one is in the form of a letter, all written during the span of his ministry. He wrote them over his three missionary journeys throughout Asia Minor and Greece from the years 47 AD to his imprisonment in Rome around 60 AD. Many letters were written to the churches he established along the way, as is the case for 1 and 2 Thessalonians. His last three letters were more personally written to brothers in Christ, Philemon and Timothy. It is widely believed 1 and 2 Thessalonians are some of the first letters Paul wrote to a newly formed, young church in Thessalonica.

All of Paul's letters, whether corporate or personal, share a common thread. They all are a testament to the truth and power of the gospel of Jesus Christ. Paul knew that power well. He experienced it. He lived it, breathed it, and placed his hope for the future in it. The gospel of Jesus Christ defined his life, at least it did after one day on the Damascus Road. Before that divine moment, Paul was a completely different person. He was known to many as Saul of Tarsus, the man who hated and persecuted Christians.

Caught Up in the World

Maybe that's the Paul you're familiar with. The book of Acts gives us Paul's conversion story. We'll be overlapping chapters in Acts with some of this study so you can see all the details happening behind the scenes in 1 & 2 Thessalonians. If you were to peek into Paul's earlier life in Acts 7–9, you would encounter the man known as Saul speaking death threats against anyone following Jesus; hatred fueling each step. On that day described in Acts 9, Saul was headed for Damascus to drag any and all Christians back to Jerusalem to stand trial before the Sanhedrin. How dare anyone put their faith in Jesus and follow Him?

Caught Up in Christ

However, everything radically changed as Saul traveled a dusty dirt road leading out of Jerusalem to Damascus. The risen Lord met Saul and interrupted his life. His sinful heart was exposed and his motives laid bare. Saul, later known as Paul, met his Savior, seeing Jesus with unveiled, fresh eyes. He would never be the same. Saved from a life of destruction, Paul now lived for God, building His kingdom. You could say from his divine Damascus Road conversion, Paul's life was "caught up" in the life of Christ. No longer consumed with a worldly lifestyle, prestige, religiosity, or self-righteousness, Paul surrendered his life to Christ's power and influence; he lived only for Christ. How could anyone not put their faith in Jesus and follow Him?

Life Before Christ; Life with Christ

The change didn't happen overnight. It often doesn't for most of us. The sanctifying work of the Holy Spirit is a gradual process. Paul touches on this in Thessalonians. For Paul, there was a defining moment in his life when he put his faith in Jesus instead of trusting in his own power and strength. Despite Paul's Jewish education under the highly esteemed Jewish Rabbi Gamaliel, his Roman citizenship and influential Greek instruction, Paul knew all of that meant nothing compared to the excellence of the knowledge of Christ Jesus his Lord (Philippians 3:8a). He recognized he was a sinner, calling himself the chief of all sinners, and had no confidence in his flesh to save him or sanctify him. But just as it was a process for Paul, it is a process for each of us. Even after Paul left Damascus, he spent three years in Arabia (Galatians 1:17–18) before going back to Jerusalem. He eventually went with Barnabas to the city of Antioch where his evangelistic ministry began to flourish. During those three years in the Arabian desert, it seems the Lord worked in Paul's heart—his life was transformed, his priorities were reordered, and he desired to learn more about Christ.

> FOR PAUL, THERE WAS A DEFINING MOMENT IN HIS LIFE WHEN HE PUT HIS FAITH IN JESUS INSTEAD OF TRUSTING IN HIS OWN POWER AND STRENGTH.

Paul's Purpose for Writing 1 & 2 Thessalonians

We all must have this moment when we choose to put our faith in Jesus and receive His payment for our sin. It is the starting point of a newly forgiven life in Christ. Often it is that very place where Paul starts most of his letters, including 1 & 2 Thessalonians. It is widely held that Paul wrote 1 and 2 Thessalonians from Corinth around 50–51 AD; about 20 years after Jesus' death, burial, and resurrection. Having traveled to the city of Thessalonica from Philippi on his second missionary journey with Silas and Timothy, Paul preached Christ to the Thessalonians. His message was received by some, and a church was birthed. Those who opposed the truth of Jesus started an uprising in Thessalonica against Paul. Under the cover of night, Paul, Silas, and Timothy escaped to the neighboring town of Berea. In this lesson, you will look at these events more closely from Acts 17.

Paul sent Timothy back to Thessalonica a few months later to check on the young church. Timothy brought word to Paul that the Thessalonian believers were standing strong in their faith despite ongoing persecution. Many had questions about the Lord's return for themselves and those who had previously died.

From Corinth, Paul penned his letters to this small church in Thessalonica to reaffirm their faith, answer some of their questions, and exhort them in the essentials of Christian living. In his letters to the Thessalonians, unlike his other letters, Paul reminds the church that the greatest hope we have is eternal life with Jesus in heaven. The time is coming when the trumpet will sound, and believers will be "caught up" in the clouds when Jesus returns. With this hope in mind, Paul writes to remind us, too, to stand strong in the Lord as we wait for Him.

WHAT ABOUT YOU?

When did you first encounter Jesus? What roads were you traveling when He met you? Do the things that once captured your attention hold less importance now? As we open the pages of 1 and 2 Thessalonians, let's get caught up in Jesus together; who He is, and all that He has for us.

Open in Prayer

Prepare your heart before studying by filling in the prayer prompts and praying them back to the Lord as you begin.

God, You are…

God, forgive me…

God, thank You for…

God, please help me…

RECEIVING GOD'S WORD

Read 1 Thessalonians 1:1; 2 Thessalonians 1:1; Acts 17:1–15

Experiencing God's Word

EXPERIENCE 1

AUTHOR AND MINISTRY PARTNERS IN THESSALONICA

---

1 Thessalonians 1:1 and 2 Thessalonians 1:1 introduce Paul, the author of the letters, and his companions Silvanus (Silas) and Timothy. We will also examine some verses in Acts for additional context as we learn more about each of these people.

Paul

1. You learned a bit about Paul (Saul of Tarsus) in the introduction. Read the verses below that testify about his character. What else do you learn about Paul from the following verses?

    - Acts 20:23–24

    - Galatians 1:15–16

Silvanus (Silas)

2. In 1 Thessalonians 1:1 and 2 Thessalonians 1:1 Paul introduces a co-worker named Silvanus (Silas). Scripture doesn't give us a lot of information regarding Silas. We know from 1 Peter 5:12 that Silas later served with Peter, which demonstrates Silas had a far-reaching scope of ministry. Read the verses below and note what you learn about Silas' ministry alongside Paul.

    - Acts 15:22

    - Acts 15:36–41

Timothy

3. While Paul was in Athens, Timothy returned to Thessalonica to check on the Thessalonians' spiritual state. These letters were written because of Timothy's report to Paul. Timothy's faith was established under the upbringing of his mother and grandmother (2 Timothy 1:1–5). It is believed that Timothy became a follower of Jesus during Paul's first missionary trip to Lystra in Acts 14:6,19. In Acts 16, Paul brings Silas with him and heads back to the towns of Derbe and Lystra on his second missionary journey. Upon arrival, they meet Timothy. What do you learn about Timothy in Acts 16:1–5?

4. Paul and Timothy had a close relationship. One of Paul's final letters was written to Timothy from prison. While Paul was in Macedonia, he wrote his first letter to Timothy who was in Ephesus. Read 1 Timothy 4:12–16. Describe Paul's urging to Timothy as a fellow worker for the gospel. These urgings summarize Paul's message throughout his evangelistic ministry.

   a. How does Paul address Timothy's age regarding ministry? (v. 12)

   b. What things should Timothy be concerned with or "caught up" in? Why? (v. 13–16)

EXPERIENCE 2

BACKGROUND ON PAUL AND THE THESSALONIANS

1. Below is a map of the area in Asia Minor where Paul established churches. Based on Acts 18:1, it is believed Paul was in Corinth when he wrote to the Thessalonians during his second missionary journey (50–51 AD). Circle Thessalonica and Corinth on the map.

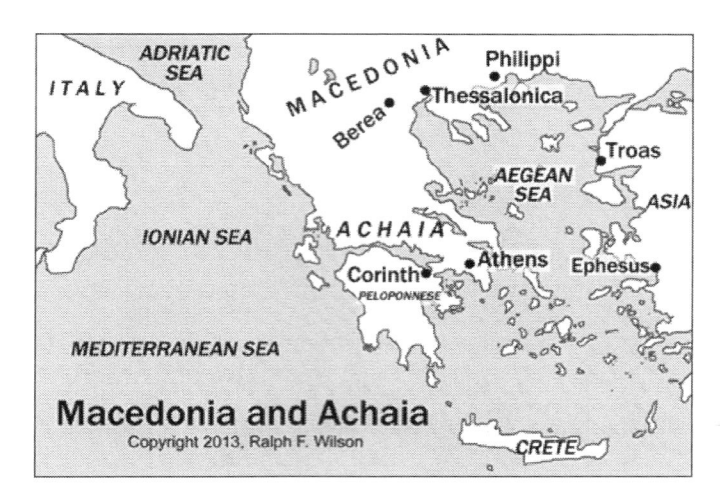

DEEPER EXPERIENCE

> "Unlike many New Testament cities, Thessalonica still exists and flourishes today. It is in northeastern Greece. In Paul's time, it was home to about 200,000 people. It was set at the junction of two major trade routes and had a fine harbor. It provides a good example of how Paul chose strategic locations for his ministry. Thessalonica drew many visitors and travelers from a wide area; those who responded to the gospel there would take it wherever they traveled (1 Thessalonians 1:8)." (CLC Bible Companion, p. 361–362)

2. Acts 17 describes Paul's time in Thessalonica with Silas and Timothy. He was there for three Sabbaths (Acts 17:2). Read Acts 17:1–15 to gain further understanding of Paul's ministry to the Thessalonians. Why did Paul's ministry end in Thessalonica?

3. Based on what you just learned in Acts 17 about the Thessalonians, summarize the state of this young church and its people after Paul departs. Take note of verse 11 comparing the Bereans with the young Thessalonian believers.

Acting on God's Word

Paul, the author of 1 and 2 Thessalonians, was a man who personified God's transforming power. As we learned in the opening pages of this week's lesson, he went from being "caught up" in the things of this world, to being "caught up" in Jesus Christ. Paul, who was previously known as Saul of Tarsus, had an encounter with God on the road to Damascus. Before this encounter, his life had been consumed by such things as religious legalism, pride, and the persecution of the church. However, after his conversion experience, he gradually began to immerse himself full-time in teaching and exhorting both the Jews and the Gentiles. Paul's life mission became sharing the good news of Jesus' life, death, and resurrection. His life reflected that he had been truly born again into a new life and new identity. Paul's life was so transformed that by the time he wrote the book of Philippians, he would say, "But what things were gain to me, these I have counted loss for Christ." What once defined him was of no value compared to knowing and serving the Lord (Philippians 3:7–10).

> PAUL'S LIFE MISSION BECAME SHARING THE GOOD NEWS OF JESUS' LIFE, DEATH, AND RESURRECTION.

When you consider the title of this Bible study, *Caught Up*, what comes to your mind? Are you, like Saul or Paul, caught up in the things of this world or the things of God? As believers, we each have a defining moment when we choose to accept Jesus Christ as our Savior. That salvation moment changes everything because Christ has shattered our darkness with His light of truth. This is a glorious day for a Christian.

Yet, this is only the first step in a lifelong journey. As our faith in Jesus grows, the Holy Spirit, who is given to us on the day of our salvation, guides us through the sanctification process. The more we learn about Christ, the more His priorities become our priorities. Our behaviors change because we desire to please God more than ourselves. The things of this world lose their luster and gradually fade because things of heaven become sharper and in focus.

Are you new to studying your Bible? Perhaps you have never put your faith in Jesus and have yet to decide to follow Him. The Bible teaches that everyone falls short of God's perfect requirements (Romans 3:23), and therefore, we all need to be forgiven by God for the things we have done wrong. If you have never taken this step, please turn to the "Delighting in My Salvation" section of your workbook and read how to ask God to forgive you and begin a restored relationship with Him. If you take this step, please tell someone! Your small group leader would love to celebrate this decision with you. If you have taken this step, praise God for your new life in Christ.

Each of us has our own unique faith story. In the questions below, we will take some time to consider yours as well as those we learned about in the lesson.

1. When you consider the title of this Bible study, *Caught Up*, what comes to your mind? Write your thoughts below.

2. What were you "caught up" with before your profession of faith in Jesus Christ?

   a. Is there ever a tendency to want the lifestyle you described in your "before Christ" life? If so, describe how you are managing that struggle.

3. How did your life begin to change after your profession of faith in Jesus Christ?

4. How does your relationship with Christ fill your desire for the things in this world?

5. Is there an area in your life where you would like to be "caught up" more with Christ and "caught up" less in the world? Describe the change you would like to see occur.

DELIGHTING IN GOD'S WORD

GET CAUGHT UP IN SCRIPTURE

Throughout this study, we will consider what it means to be caught up in Christ or caught up in the things of this world. One of the best ways to keep our minds "caught up" in Christ is to memorize scripture.

If you turn to the back of your workbook, you will find a Scripture Memory Cards page with eight scripture references printed for you. Remove this page from your workbook and cut the eight cards apart. (You may want to glue them onto cardstock or 3 x 5 notecards to make them more durable.) Once you have done this, place the cards where you will remember to study them regularly over the next eight weeks. After each weekly lesson, we will ask you to memorize one of the verses found on the scripture memory cards. The goal will be to memorize all eight verses by the time you finish the study.

Close in Prayer

WEEK 2

CAUGHT UP IN THE GOSPEL

As you begin reading Paul's letter to the Thessalonians, it is hard to miss his love for this precious group of new believers. He remembers them fondly. Although his time with them was brief, it must have been sweet because the tone of his letter sounds like words coming from a loving friend. He begins by greeting them in the powerful name of Jesus and then expresses how he has been praying for them diligently since fleeing from their city for his safety. He praises them for their steadfastness in their faith despite persecution and the hardships they endured. He goes on to thank God for their influence upon others who have come to know Christ through their good example and testimony. He is pleased to learn their lives have been impacting others in the region through their faith, love, and hope. The gospel was going forth, and people were turning from their sinful ways, serving God, and looking forward to the day of Christ's return. Paul's ministry, which was to fulfill the great commission Jesus gave in Matthew 28:19–20, was happening. The truth about Jesus Christ was going forth, and Paul's enthusiasm is contagious as you read his words to the Thessalonians in chapter one.

The Thessalonian church reminds me a little bit of what it is like when a pebble is dropped into a pond. Although it is small, its impact on the water is great. Although the pebble disappears, ripples quickly begin to grow outward from where the pebble was dropped into the water. First, one ring appears, then quickly another ring forms further out, and then another follows until the rippling effect reaches the edge of the pond.

> THE GOSPEL WAS GOING FORTH, AND PEOPLE WERE TURNING FROM THEIR SINFUL WAYS, SERVING GOD, AND LOOKING FORWARD TO THE DAY OF CHRIST'S RETURN.

Much like a pebble dropped into a pond, the Thessalonians were engulfed and caught up by the truth of the gospel which Paul had taught them. Its rippling effect was still spreading out toward the edges of the pond as more and more people began to hear about Christ's life, death, and resurrection. Although it was certainly a difficult time to be a Christian, it was also an exciting one, too, because the truth of Jesus was transforming. Now there was a way to make peace with God and be assured of an eternity with Him. That news was powerful, hope-filled, and contagious.

As you begin your time of study, consider how your life has been impacted by the gospel from its first day until now. Where have you, like the early church in Thessalonica, seen a rippling effect of your faith in the lives of other people? In what ways have your faith, hope, and love grown toward the Lord and away from your life of the past? As you think about these things, you are entering a headspace similar to Paul's when he wrote to this young church because he had these things on his mind as well. Join him now on the pages of Scripture as you open up your Bible to the book of 1 Thessalonians.

Open in Prayer

Prepare your heart before studying by filling in the prayer prompts and praying them back to the Lord as you begin.

God, You are…

God, forgive me…

God, thank You for…

God, please help me…

RECEIVING GOD'S WORD

Read 1 Thessalonians 1

EXPERIENCING GOD'S WORD

- Greeting (1:1)
- Prayer (1:2)
- Thanking God for their faith, love, and hope (1:3-5)
- Thessalonians' conversion (1:6-10)

EXPERIENCE 1 (10 minutes)

OBSERVATION OF 1 THESSALONIANS 1:1–10

The following verse-by-verse questions are to help you get a broad understanding of the chapter. The answers will be found directly in the text.

1. How does Paul greet the church in Thessalonica in verse 1?

DEEPER EXPERIENCE

> "The expression 'the church…which is in God the Father and the Lord Jesus Christ' is peculiar to the Thessalonians letters. Of course, it refers to the same church that is elsewhere spoken of as 'the body of Christ,' but here the emphasis is on the new relationship into which these young Christians have come. They were now linked in infinite grace with God the Father; they were His children. They owed their position in the family of God to the Lord Jesus Christ, who had given Himself for them." (Ironside, H.A., 1 & 2 Thessalonians, p. 18)

2. When Paul prays for the Thessalonians, what does he remember about them in verses 2–4?

DEEPER EXPERIENCE

> "The word rendered 'church' (ekklēsia) was a familiar nonreligious term among the Greeks. Composed of the preposition ek (out of) and the substantive form of the verb kaleō (to call), the term quite literally means 'a called-out company.' When the Jewish nation forfeited its prerogative of being the distinctive people of God through its rejection of the Messiah, the believers in Jesus Christ carried on the claim to be the true ekklēsia, the Christian church." (Hiebert, D. Edmond, 1 & 2 Thessalonians, p. 41)

3. According to verse 6, what was the life of the young believers like when they heard the gospel? What words give you this impression?

4. Use verses 7–8 to describe the power of the young church's testimony.

5. What proof is given in verses 9–10 that the Thessalonians were genuine believers?

6. Summarize broadly what is happening in verses 1–10.

7. What do you learn about God's character from these verses?

CONSIDER

Consider Paul's personal walk with God and its impact on the Thessalonians. A person's faith in God has the potential to touch many lives. What do you see in Paul's relationship with Jesus that influenced the lives of the Thessalonians and others? Write your thoughts below.

_____

_____

_____

_____

EXPERIENCE 2 (15 minutes)

THANKING GOD FOR THEIR FAITH, HOPE, AND LOVE
1 Thessalonians 1:2–5

If you recall from last week's lesson, Paul and Silas had to quickly leave Thessalonica in the middle of the night. They were run out of town by Jewish enemies of the gospel. Paul was greatly concerned about the persecution facing the new Christian converts he left behind. However, he was relieved after hearing of their well-being during great affliction. Let's dig into verses 2–5 to look at the faith, hope, and love of the Thessalonians.

1. In verse 3 Paul connects three God-given gifts (faith, love, and hope) with three outward manifestations (work, labor, and patience/endurance) in the life of a believer; one should result from the other. Read how the New International Version of the Bible words this verse: *"We continually remember before our God and Father your work produced by faith, your labor prompted by love, and your endurance inspired by hope in our Lord Jesus Christ."*
Fill in the blank below with the outworking of faith.

    Faith produces_____

    a. Read Ephesians 2:8–10. What do these verses say about faith and works?

WEEK 2: CAUGHT UP IN THE GOSPEL | 25

b. Read James 2:14–20. Describe the relationship between faith and works.

2. The next spiritual gift Paul recognizes is the Thessalonians' love. Fill in the blank below with the outworking of love from 1 Thessalonians 1:3.

Love prompts _____

a. Read 1 Corinthians 13:4–8a. Describe how love is a labor from these verses.

b. Is the work spiritual, physical, or both? Explain.

3. Lastly, Paul addresses the Thessalonians' hopeful perspective during hardship. What does he pair with their hope?

Hope inspires _____

a. Read 1 Peter 1:3–4. Describe the basis for a believer's hope and how this kind of hope should keep us going despite hard times.

b. Read Hebrews 6:9–12 and 19–20. Why is hope just as important as faith and love for a believer?

4. In 1 Thessalonians 1:4 Paul mentions the election of God in the lives of the Thessalonian believers. The doctrine of God's election can stir up questions and difficulties among different denominations and Christian theologies. Election is woven throughout the Bible from God choosing the Jewish nation to God choosing those who will put their faith in Him through Jesus. God's heart is for all people to be saved through Jesus (John 3:16, 1 John 4:10). We also know that God created each of us with the ability to choose. We must choose to trust in Jesus and accept His payment for our sins (Romans 10:9–10). When we do, we are part of God's chosen people, His elect. Read Ephesians 1:3–6. Based on these verses and 1 Thessalonians 1:2–5, why would Paul make mention of election alongside the topic of faith, love, and hope?

5. Use Thessalonians 1:5 to describe the tools of evangelism Paul used with the Thessalonians.

CONSIDER

Consider Paul's prayer for the Thessalonians in verses 2–5. How did Paul's prayer show that he, too, lived a life of faith, love, and hope?

_____

_____

_____

_____

WEEK 2: CAUGHT UP IN THE GOSPEL | 27

EXPERIENCE 3 (15 minutes)

THESSALONIANS' RESPONSE TO THE GOSPEL
1 Thessalonians 2:6–10

In this section, we will pick up in verse 6 and read through verse 10. These verses explain what resulted when the Thessalonians received the gospel.

1. In Week 1 we examined Acts 17 extensively; however, let's go there once again to look at how Paul preached the gospel. Read Acts 17:1–4. What were the two main points Paul made about Jesus when he preached to the Thessalonians?

2. When someone accepts the gospel, their life should reflect their decision. Read 1 Thessalonians 1:6–7. The Thessalonians became an example to everyone in Macedonia and Achaia amid being persecuted. List a few ways the Thessalonians' example would have been a powerful testimony.

DEEPER EXPERIENCE

> "The following verses [v.5–6] explain why Paul was so confident in knowing the Thessalonians are God's elect. In a sermon on 1 Thessalonians 1:5–6, Charles Spurgeon found four pieces of evidence of election:
>
> - The Word of God coming home with power (our gospel did not come to you in word only, but also in power).
> - The reception of God's Word with much assurance (and in much assurance).
> - The desire to be like Jesus (you became followers of us and of the Lord).
> - The existence of spiritual joy in spiritual service (in much affliction, with joy of the Holy Spirit)." (David Guzik, www.blueletterbible.org)

3. Read 1 Thessalonians 1:8. After the people in Thessalonica put their faith in Jesus, as verse 8 says, "the word of the Lord [had] sounded forth" to the nearby communities. What impact did their testimony have on Paul's ministry? If their testimony sounded forth differently, how could it have hindered Paul's ministry?

4. Read 1 Thessalonians 1:9–10. There is a progression found in these verses in response to the gospel. The people turned, served, and waited. How do these three words cover the whole Christian life from beginning to end?

    a. Based on verse 10, how does the gospel deliver/rescue us while also inspiring hope?

DEEPER EXPERIENCE

> "The moral standards of the Thessalonians, the majority of whom were idolaters, were certainly no higher than those in any ordinary Greek city. Thessalonica never acquired a reputation for immorality like Corinth, yet immoral practices were frightfully common in its idolatrous society. The effects of the paganism that clutched its inhabitants were truly degrading." (Hiebert, D. Edmond, *1 & 2 Thessalonians*, p. 16)

5. It wasn't only the Thessalonians who changed after meeting Paul. Read Acts 16:25–34 to learn about another person and his family who were impacted by the gospel. Then answer the following questions.

    a. What were Paul and Silas doing while they were bound up in prison? (v. 25)

    b. What did the jailer want to know? (v. 30)

c. Summarize Paul's gospel message. (v. 31–32)

d. How does the jailer exemplify <u>turning</u>, <u>sounding forth</u>, and <u>serving</u> in response to the gospel in these verses?

CONSIDER

Consider how the gospel message changed the lives of Thessalonians through the example of Paul and his co-laborers. How did the Thessalonians then become an example to their generation? How are they still an example for us today? What does this reveal about the power of the word of God?

_____

_____

_____

_____

ACTING ON GOD'S WORD

The young church in Thessalonica shows us how the power of the gospel can impact the life of one person as well as the lives of many. As we saw in this chapter, when one Thessalonian became caught up in the gospel, many lives were affected within Thessalonica which then spread outward into neighboring communities.

Paul, Silas, and Timothy were evangelists, but so were the people in the newly formed church, and they probably didn't even realize they had a new role in their community. How about you?

1. Do you actively think about sharing the gospel with others? Do you look for opportunities? Why or why not? Share an example of when you were able to share the gospel.

2. When you think of witnessing to others, does anything hinder you from sharing? If so, what?

3. How might 1 Thessalonians 1 encourage you regarding the mission of evangelism as well as your approach? Explain.

4. Think about the people in your immediate life (family and friends) as well as those around you (neighborhood, workplace, gym, or regular stores you shop). List names of people or specific places where you have opportunities to share the gospel of Jesus with others. Pray over the list and ask God to give you boldness and for hearts prepared to receive Him as He gives you opportunities to share.

5. In verses 1–10 Paul gave many examples of how the Thessalonians' lives sounded forth the gospel. Those examples are listed below. Which ones come most easily to you? Which ones are harder? Circle the easy ones and put a star next to the hard areas. As you close in prayer, ask God to help you in the areas you starred.

Work of faith	Obedient to God	Trust in God
Labor of love	Receptive to instruction	Manner of living/holiness
Patience of hope	Joyful in difficult times	Serve God

DELIGHTING IN GOD'S WORD

GET CAUGHT UP IN SCRIPTURE

In Week 1 you were directed to cut apart the eight scripture memory cards which are found in the back of your workbook. If you have not done so, please do it now. If you have already cut apart the cards, please locate those cards.

Read Week 2's memory verse. Next write the verse below to encourage your memorization of it, and then place the card somewhere you will see it throughout the week.

1 Thessalonians 1:5

Try to memorize the verses on all eight memory cards by the time you finish the study.

Close in Prayer

WEEK 2: CAUGHT UP IN THE GOSPEL

Teaching Title _____

Teaching Videos and handouts are available for free at www.delightinginthelord.com.

WEEK 2: CAUGHT UP IN THE GOSPEL

Teaching Title _____

Teaching Videos and handouts are available for free at www.delightinginthelord.com.

WEEK 3

CAUGHT UP IN PLEASING GOD

Paul was no stranger to opposition. Having been an antagonist to the gospel for so long, once he became a believer, he quickly learned what it was like to be on the receiving end of that kind of hatred. As a follower of Jesus and a minister of the gospel throughout Asia Minor, Paul's motives were continually called into question, his teachings were rejected, and many enemies were formed against him.

Just before Paul came to Thessalonica, you may recall that he and Silas were falsely accused of troubling the people in Philippi and teaching erroneous customs. As a result, the local magistrate ordered their imprisonment. Even so, they weren't dissuaded. They knew their heart motivations were right before the Lord. Despite ongoing opposition, their aim in each town was to share the gospel of Jesus Christ, neither for personal gain nor profit. It was the gospel's power that brought them to Thessalonica with their wrists still bearing the marks of the shackles, but it was Paul's steadfast heart for Jesus that made him care for the lost, burdened for new believers, and speak truth again and again.

> PAUL ALLOWED GOD TO TEST HIS HEART; TO SIFT THROUGH WHAT WAS HIS MOTIVE AND WHAT WAS GOD'S.

As we open 1 Thessalonians 2, we'll see Paul defending his intentions and motivations. He confidently writes he didn't come from "error, uncleanness, or deceit" (1 Thessalonians 2:3b). He declared he was "approved by God to be entrusted with the gospel" (1 Thessalonians 2:4). How could he say this? It wasn't because of his background, education, or even the things he had accomplished. And that's saying a lot coming from Paul. It was all because of Jesus, and Paul's heart was set on pleasing Him. God had preeminence in his life. As a result, Paul allowed God to test his heart; to sift through what was his motive and what was God's. He put his choices and intentions under the exposure of God's truth.

When thinking about the hidden and exposed, photography comes to mind. Before smartphones and digital photos, taking a photograph wasn't as easy as it is today. Back then you needed a camera and film. The inner workings of the camera captured a picture at the click of a button, but that image could only be revealed through the developing process. That process exposed the picture held deep in the flimsy roll of film. Some of you may remember putting a little roll of 35mm film in an envelope and sending it away for processing. Then you waited, hoping the glossy prints would give evidence of the beautiful images you thought you captured. When the 24 or 36 photo prints were returned to you by postal mail, you finally saw what the pictures really looked like. You saw the flaws, the photobombs, the blurred images, and the missed photo opportunities. But you also saw the beautifully captured moments.

That's what it is like when we allow God to test our hearts and expose our motives. He reveals the true picture of our hearts. He shows us the dark places of greed, pride, selfishness, covetousness, and people-pleasing. He shows what is done in our fleshly desires and what is done in His Spirit and character. This spiritual tug of war will continue in us until we see the Lord face to face in glory. Paul knew the battle waged by Satan well, as Satan tried to hinder God's work in Paul again and again. I'm sure each of us knows this battle well too. As we study 1 Thessalonians 2, may we let God look within our hearts and expose the places of sin. May it be our aim, as it was Paul's, to be caught up in pleasing God.

Open in Prayer

Prepare your heart before studying by filling in the prayer prompts and praying them back to the Lord as you begin.

God, You are…

God, forgive me…

God, thank You for…

God, please help me…

RECEIVING GOD'S WORD

Read 1 Thessalonians 2

EXPERIENCING GOD'S WORD

Paul's behavior and heart toward the Thessalonians (2:1-12) → The Thessalonians' conduct and persecution (2:13-16) → Paul's desire to be with the Thessalonians (2:17-20)

EXPERIENCE 1 (15 minutes)

OBSERVATION OF 1 THESSALONIANS 2:1–20

Below are verse-by-verse questions to help you get a broad understanding of the chapter. The answers will be found directly in the text.

1. Read 1 Thessalonians 2:1–2. Describe the situation Paul, Silas, and Timothy encountered when they came to the Thessalonians.

2. Read 1 Thessalonians 2:3–4. What was the heart motivation of Paul and his companions when they appealed to the Thessalonians?

3. Use verses 5–9 to list all the ungodly motivations that Paul and his companions could have used when they shared the gospel with the Thessalonians.

4. Use verses 10–11 to explain how Paul presented the gospel.

5. Verse 12 tells us Paul's goal in sharing the gospel with the Thessalonians. What was it?

6. Paul is so thankful for the Thessalonians, so much so that he thanks God for them. Why is he thankful in verse 13?

7. According to verses 14–16, how are the Thessalonians like the Jewish believers in Judea? Who specifically hindered the gospel?

8. Based on verse 17, what is Paul's heart longing for regarding the Thessalonians?

9. Who in verse 18 hindered Paul from being with the Thessalonians?

10. What does Paul say in verses 19–20 that encourages the Thessalonians' Christian walk while they are facing persecution?

11. Summarize broadly what is happening in verses 1–20.

12. What did you learn about God's character from these verses?

CONSIDER

Consider Paul's motives and how his outward actions supported his inner motivation. Write your thoughts below.

_____

_____

_____

_____

EXPERIENCE 2 (15 minutes)

PURE INTENTIONS THAT PLEASE GOD
1 Thessalonians 2:1–12

Intentions matter. Very simply, an intention is something we aim at with determination to achieve it. Said another way, an intention starts inward and finishes outward. To get at the heart, we all must ask ourselves, "What is my motivation?" "Why do I do the things I do?" In 1 Thessalonians 2, Paul, Silas, and Timothy had pure reasons for coming to the Thessalonians. They were for kingdom-building purposes, and we are told ultimately to please God. Let's look at Paul's example of how to live a life for God.

1. In Experience 2 of last week's lesson, you looked at the Philippian jailor who received Jesus as his Lord and Savior while Paul and Silas were imprisoned. Despite the conflict that put them in jail, 1 Thessalonians 2:1–2 tells us they came to Thessalonica from Philippi bruised and battered, yet boldly sharing the gospel. How was Paul able to live with such God-focused intentions despite ongoing persecution and false accusations? Read the following verses and note what you learn.

    - Matthew 22:37–40

    - 2 Corinthians 5:15

    - Romans 12:1–2

    - Romans 8:28

WEEK 3: CAUGHT UP IN PLEASING GOD | 39

2. In 1 Thessalonians 2:3–12, Paul reminds the Thessalonians of his actions toward them. Use these verses to fill in the two columns below.

List what were his actions/words	List what were not his actions/words

3. Read Ephesians 4:17–31. The behavior of the Ephesians is very similar to the list you made in the previous question. Two types of people are presented in Ephesians 4:17–31. Use these verses to compare the two kinds of people and their behaviors.

DEEPER EXPERIENCE

"As to their moral standards, the Thessalonians were hardly any different from the citizens of any other large Greek city. Presumably, most were idolaters, though it is certain that some were seeking a different kind of religious experience than polytheism could provide; hence, they attached themselves (loosely) to the local synagogue." (Bible.org)

4. Read the verses that describe the life that pleases God. Fill in the blanks with a word that summarizes what the verse is saying.

   1 Samuel 15:22 The Lord delights in our _____ to Him.

   Psalm 147:11 The Lord takes pleasure in those who _____ _____.

   Romans 8:6–8 Those in the _____ cannot please God.

   Hebrews 11:6 Without _____ we cannot please God.

   Hebrews 13:15–16 God is well pleased with our _____ of praise.

5. Paul uses the example of parenting in verse 7 to describe his care for the Thessalonians. How does his analogy express his complete love and concern for them?

6. How can Paul confidently say his intentions in verses 3–12 were pure and pleasing to God?

CONSIDER

Consider how Paul's words, actions, approach, and expectations ultimately modeled Jesus. This should be an example for each of us. As you consider this, note your thoughts below.

_____

_____

_____

_____

WEEK 3: CAUGHT UP IN PLEASING GOD | 41

EXPERIENCE 3 (15 minutes)

THE ONE BEHIND IMPURE INTENTIONS
1 Thessalonians 2:13–20

In Experience 2 you examined how Paul did his best to serve God with pure intentions. However, pleasing God can sometimes be difficult when our fleshly desires take over. Selfishness, personal gratification, and impure motives do not please God. Even the most devout Christian must be ready to fight this spiritual battle. Satan is the adversary to God and believers. Scripture tells us that Satan is a liar, a thief, and a roaring lion who seeks to devour believers (1 Peter 5:8, John 10:10, John 8:44). He harasses, tempts, and tries to oppress those who have put their faith in God (Matthew 4:1). However, if we step back and examine what is happening when we feel tempted to do things we know are not godly, it shouldn't take long to recognize Satan is the one creating havoc against those who are trying to please God.

---

1. Below is the New King James Version of 1 Thessalonians 2:14–16, 18. Read it and complete the prompts under the verses.

   ¹⁴"For you, brethren, became imitators of the churches of God which are in Judea in Christ Jesus. For you also suffered the same things from your own countrymen, just as they *did* from the Judeans, who killed both the Lord Jesus and their own prophets, and have persecuted us; and they do not please God and are contrary to all men, forbidding us to speak to the Gentiles that they may be saved, so as always to fill up *the measure* of their sins; but wrath has come upon them to the uttermost. ¹⁸Therefore we wanted to come to you—even I, Paul, time and again—but Satan hindered us."

   a. Circle those who are trying to please God.

   b. Underline those who are behaving with impure motives.

   c. Put a zigzag line under words that describe behaviors that are unpleasing to God.

   d. Put a double line under the judgment to come for those who will not repent of their sins.

2. Read Luke 22:31–32. Describe what Satan wanted to do to Peter. Why would he want to do this? Think of Satan's intentions.

   a. How is this similar to what Satan was trying to do to the Thessalonians, Paul, and Jesus in 1 Thessalonians 2:14–16,18?

   b. Describe the encouragement Jesus gives Peter in Luke 22:32. How is Paul doing the same thing for the believers in Thessalonica?

3. Read Acts 9:4–5. How does Jesus describe hostility toward the church?

4. Read Ephesians 6:10–12. Describe the warfare of believers.

   a. Read 1 John 5:19. Who has a measure of control in the world today?

   b. With what you just learned, how might 1 Thessalonians 2:18 explain why Paul believed it was Satan who hindered him from going back to see the Thessalonians?

WEEK 3: CAUGHT UP IN PLEASING GOD | 43

5. Read 1 Peter 2:21–24, 5:6–9. During difficulty, describe what we can do to keep our intentions and actions pure.

6. Go back to 1 Thessalonians 2:13. How were the Thessalonian believers able to withstand the outward oppression happening in their lives? What is the difference between the words "received" and "welcomed" in verse 13? Why is this important regarding our motivations and actions?

CONSIDER

Consider and comment on how Paul overcame the many ways Satan tried to work against him.

_____

_____

_____

_____

Acting on God's Word

When Paul, Timothy, and Silas came to the Thessalonians, their words and actions testified to Christ's transforming power. Their intentions were proven pure, and Paul reminded the Thessalonians of how they behaved when they lived among them (v. 3–12). However, despite their upright lives, persecution and accusations followed them. Paul spent most of 1 Thessalonians 2 defending his character and ministry, all while trusting that God knew his heart.

> AS A FOLLOWER OF JESUS CHRIST, YOUR INTENTIONS MATTER. GOD CARES ABOUT WHAT WE DO AND WHY WE DO IT.

As a follower of Jesus Christ, your intentions matter. God cares about what we do and why we do it. He wants to show us what is in our hearts as He sees the motivations behind our actions. One day God will reward those who have had pure, godly motives in how they lived their lives for Christ alone. (1 Corinthians 3 and 4:5). Answer the following question to examine your motives for the work you do unto the Lord.

1. Read the statements below. Put a check next to any statement you struggle to do with a pure heart motivation unto the Lord.

    _____ When I must sacrifice to give my money or time.
    _____ When I work or serve, and no one seems to notice or appreciate.
    _____ When I'm asked to do something that I don't enjoy.
    _____ When I am criticized or treated harshly for doing what is right.
    _____ When I find people annoying or difficult.
    _____ When there is no evidence of success compared to others doing the same thing.
    _____ When…_____
    (fill in your own answer)

2. We only deceive ourselves if we think God doesn't notice our motives. For those statements you checked in the previous question, identify what sin might cause you to serve your own motivations or fall into the trap of pleasing ourselves and not God. Be honest with yourself (and God).

3. One way to correct our heart motivation is found in Galatians 5:16 which says, "Walk in the Spirit and you shall not fulfill the lust of the flesh." What does it mean to walk in the Spirit? How does the Spirit correct you and give you the ability to change your attitude?

4. End by writing a prayer asking God to forgive you and help you in any areas you identified above where you have been caught up in pleasing yourself instead of God.

Delighting in God's Word

GET CAUGHT UP IN SCRIPTURE

Read Week 3's memory verse from the cards you cut apart from the back of your workbook. Next, write the verse below to encourage your memorization of it, and then place the card somewhere you will see it throughout the week.

1 Thessalonians 2:4

Try to memorize the verses on all eight memory cards by the time you finish the study.

Close in Prayer

WEEK 3: CAUGHT UP IN PLEASING GOD

Teaching Title _____

Teaching Videos and handouts are available for free at www.delightinginthelord.com.

WEEK 3: CAUGHT UP IN PLEASING GOD

Teaching Title _____

Teaching Videos and handouts are available for free at www.delightinginthelord.com.

WEEK 4

CAUGHT UP IN A FAITH-FILLED LIFE

Paul fulfilled two important roles Jesus laid out in the great commission (Matthew 28:19–20). He was a diligent evangelist, but he was also a teacher of God's word. Paul desired to introduce people to Christ by sharing the gospel. Once saved, he encouraged the new believers to live a life that was pleasing to God.

Paul's life exemplified what it was like to be caught up in living a faith-filled life. Everything he did was based upon his trust in Jesus. He shared the gospel, planted churches, and discipled new converts. All his actions stemmed from his love and faith in God. Having been run out of Thessalonica by Jewish opposition, Paul wanted to ensure the young Thessalonian church was established in their faith because he knew they were probably facing the same opposition. Faith in God was the great stabilizer for Paul. In writing this letter, he wanted assurance that the Thessalonians' faith was strong, too, so they could endure the hardships the evil one would bring against them.

1 Thessalonians 3 is a continuation of Paul's message from chapter 2. He reminds the fledgling church of his personal investment in their lives, despite having left abruptly. Paul wanted to encourage them, but it is their faith that concerned him most. Knowing the need for sound teaching following their conversion, he sent Timothy to see how the congregation was doing in his absence. Timothy returned with a good report, and Paul, like a concerned parent, was thrilled to learn that God had sustained their newfound faith.

> PAUL'S LIFE EXEMPLIFIED WHAT IT WAS LIKE TO BE CAUGHT UP IN LIVING A FAITH-FILLED LIFE.

The Thessalonians' faith in God could be compared to the ballast that is found on a ship. Ballast improves the stability and control of the vessel. Large ships usually have the ballast, or a ballast tank, located at the bottom of the boat. This vital material keeps the ship upright and balanced; without it, even a small wave could tip the boat.

Faith in Jesus is like ballast for a born-again Christian. It stabilizes us in difficult times and keeps us steadfast in God as we navigate life. Paul knew the importance of a rock-solid faith and used the word five times in this short chapter. He did his best to build others up in the faith so they would not be shaken. We'll see in this chapter, faith and encouragement go hand in hand. As a person walks by faith, others are encouraged in their faith. Not only did Paul encourage the Thessalonians, but he, too, was encouraged when he learned of their established faith. As you study through these verses, may your faith be steadied where it might be weak, and may you be an encouragement to those around you.

Open in Prayer

Prepare your heart before studying by filling in the prayer prompts and praying them back to the Lord as you begin.

God, You are…

God, forgive me…

God, thank You for…

God, please help me…

Receiving God's Word

Read 1 Thessalonians 3

Experiencing God's Word

- Paul's concern for the Thessalonians' faith (3:1-5)
- Paul is encouraged by the Thessalonians' faith (3:6-10)
- Paul's prayer for the Thessalonians' sanctification (3:11-13)

EXPERIENCE 1 (15 minutes)

OBSERVATION OF 1 THESSALONIANS 3:1–13

Below are verse-by-verse questions to help you get a broad understanding of the chapter. The answers will be found directly in the text.

1. It is believed in 1 Thessalonians 3:1–2 that Paul is alone in Athens. Why does Paul send Timothy back to Thessalonica?

2. What is Paul concerned about in verse 3 and how does he empathize with them?

3. Go back to 1 Thessalonians 2:14. What already happened to the believers in Thessalonica? What warning did Paul give the Thessalonians concerning their faith in 1 Thessalonians 3:4?

4. Read 1 Thessalonians 3:5. What was Paul's primary concern regarding the Thessalonians? What repeated phrase do you see in verses 2, 5, 6, 7, and 10?

5. What did Timothy report back to Paul in verse 6?

6. How did Timothy's report of the Thessalonians in verses 7–10 affect Paul?

7. Having received a good report about the Thessalonians, what does Paul pray over them in verses 11–13?

> ### CONSIDER
>
> Consider the deep love that Paul had for the Thessalonians. Back in chapter 1 verse 3, Paul made mention of the Thessalonians' "labor of love." He continues to model what that looks like in the Lord. What do you notice in verses 1–13 that demonstrates how much he cares about them?
>
> _____
> _____
> _____
> _____

EXPERIENCE 2 (25 minutes)

STEADYING FAITH
1 Thessalonians 3:1–10

Unable to bear any longer with the unknown condition of the believers in Thessalonica, Paul was willing to be left alone in Athens (Acts 17:13–15) so he could get word on the spiritual well-being of his new converts. Paul sent Timothy to the Thessalonians. Paul uses a collective thought with the word "we" in 1 Thessalonians 3:1–2, but the book of Acts implies Silas and Timothy weren't with him in Athens. They meet up with Paul sometime later in Corinth (Acts 18:5). Enduring persecution in Thessalonica, Paul knew the believers there were probably under the same affliction. Their faith needed to be strong in the Lord. Steadfast faith doesn't shine the brightest in times of ease but often will in times of struggle and pain. Was their faith holding them steady? We'll explore this question in this section.

1. In Experience 1, question 1 you identified why Paul sent Timothy to Thessalonica. He wanted Timothy to find out if their faith was established and also wanted to send them encouragement. Read 1 Thessalonians 3:1–3. Why was Paul so concerned with their faith?

2. The word used in verse 3 for *shaken* (NKJV) or *moved* (KJV) is the word *sainō* (Strong's G4525). It is used nowhere else in the New Testament. It means to wag the tail like that of a dog back and forth. Metaphorically, it refers to a person's mind that moves back and forth when agitated or troubled, like that of a dog's tail. Read James 1:2–8. Describe how James uses a similar metaphor when talking about trials and a person's faith.

   a. Paul said in 1 Thessalonians 3:3 that he was appointed to afflictions. In verse 4, Paul reminded the Thessalonian believers that suffering was a part of the Christian life, as it had been for him. Think in general about the trials and afflictions often seen in people's lives. Identify some reasons why trials can be so detrimental to a person's faith in God.

   b. Use the verses in James 1 to explain how God desires to use trials in the life of believers for beneficial reasons.

WEEK 4: CAUGHT UP IN A FAITH-FILLED LIFE | 53

3. Read Luke 6:46–49. Use the two examples given in these verses to describe the importance of having a firm foundation of faith.

4. Read 1 Thessalonians 3:5. What other reason does Paul give for sending Timothy to find out about the Thessalonians' faith?

   a. What was Paul worried might happen? Read James 1:12–15. How does James characterize Paul's fears for the Thessalonians? What was he worried might happen considering they were such new Christians?

DEEPER EXPERIENCE

> "The trials and testings that come to our lives as Christians are not accidents—they are appointments. We must expect to 'suffer for His sake' (Phil. 1:29). Persecution is not foreign to the believer (1 Peter 4:12ff), but a normal part of the Christian life. Paul had repeatedly told them this while he was with them. We must warn new believers that the way is not easy as they seek to live for Christ; otherwise, when trials come, these babes in Christ will be discouraged and defeated. Of course, behind these persecutions is Satan, the enemy of the Christian (1 Thess. 3:5). He is the tempter, and he seeks to ruin our faith." (Warren Wiersbe, The Bible Exposition Commentary: New Testament Volume 2, p.172)

DEEPER EXPERIENCE

> *"It is a stabilizing truth. The enemy cannot win in the end. And meanwhile, his worst persecutions develop character, strengthen faith, produce courage, and ensure for many believers a martyr's crown."* (John Phillips, Exploring 1 & 2 Thessalonians, p. 81)

6. Read 1 Thessalonians 3:6–9. What words convey Paul's relief upon hearing about their faith?

7. Use 1 Thessalonians 3:10 to explain what Paul hoped he, Timothy, and Silas could do for the Thessalonians' faith.

8. The word *established* in Greek is *stērizō* (Strong's G4741). It means to make firm or solid, to fix firmly in place, strengthened. Think about the stabilizer example used in the introduction. Paul desired to establish the Thessalonians' faith in God. Look up the following verses about how we can establish our faith too. Write what you learn.

    - Proverbs 3:5–6

    - Romans 10:17

    - Galatians 2:20

    - Hebrews 12:2

9. That same Greek word for *establish* used in 1 Thessalonians 3:2 regarding the Thessalonians' faith is used again in verse 13 as Paul prays for these believers. Having longed to see their faith established in God, Paul prays in verse 12 that their love will increase. What does he pray in verse 13 that God will establish in their hearts?

   a. Describe the relationship between Paul's desires for the Thessalonians seen in verses 2 and 13. How does one correlate to the other?

CONSIDER

Consider Paul's plea and prayer in 1 Thessalonians 3. What evidence do you see that Paul's life was caught up with faith in God?

_____

_____

_____

_____

EXPERIENCE 3 (20 minutes)

ENCOURAGING WORDS

1 Thessalonians 3:1–13

Proverbs 25:25 says, "As cold water to a weary soul, so is good news from a far country." This proverb may capture how Paul felt when he finally received news from Timothy about the Thessalonians' faith. He longed to know about them and was deeply encouraged by what he learned. Let's look at how the topic of encouragement is woven into this chapter.

1. Read 1 Thessalonians 3:1–5. Why was Paul in such distress (1 Thess. 2:18)? What words and phrases did he use to capture his concern?

DEEPER EXPERIENCE

> "We can imagine what it must have meant to Paul to be in Athens in utter loneliness for some time. As he walked about the streets of that great city, his heart was stirred by the idolatry he saw. All the while Paul was witnessing in Athens, he was anxious about the young Christians at Thessalonica." (H.A. Ironside, 1 & 2 Thessalonians, p. 33)

DEEPER EXPERIENCE

> "I always revel in the delightful ways Paul refers to his co-workers. Notice what he wrote in 1 Thessalonians 3:2, 'Timotheus, our brother, and minister of God and our fellow laborer in the gospel of Christ.' What more could be said of any servant of the Lord? A beloved brother in Christ, a dear fellow laborer—Timothy was all this to Paul. So he sent Timothy to establish and comfort the young Christians in Thessalonica." (H.A. Ironside, 1 & 2 Thessalonians, p. 32)

2. Read 1 Thessalonians 3:2 and 1 Timothy 4:12–13. Paul says he sent Timothy to "encourage you [the Thessalonians] concerning your faith." According to 1 Timothy 4:12–13, in what ways could Timothy encourage them in their faith? You may also include other practical ways he may have encouraged them.

3. The word *encourage* in Greek is *paraklesis* (Strong's G3874) which means to call to one's aid (para "by the side" and kaleo "to call"). It is very similar to the word Holy Spirit in Greek, *parakletos* (Strong's G3875), and its meaning. Read the following verses and note what you learn about the ways the Holy Spirit is our encouragement.

   - John 14:26

   - John 15:26

4. Read 1 Thessalonians 3:6–10. After Timothy visits the believers in Thessalonica, he reports back to Paul. Some of what Timothy shared is found in this letter. What words does Paul use to express his feelings of encouragement?

DEEPER EXPERIENCE

> "Every expression of their attachments to him [Paul] had gone to his heart, and their faith and charity had been to him in his trials the source of unspeakable consolation. His very life depended, as it were, on their fidelity, and he says he should live and be happy if they stood fast in the Lord." (Albert Barnes, *Barnes' Notes on the New Testament: Ephesians to Philemon*, p. 31)

5. As proof of his endearment, Paul ends this chapter with a sincere prayer. Read 1 Thessalonians 3:11–13. From this prayer, list the petitions Paul makes to God on behalf of the Thessalonians. Why are these requests encouraging?

6. The Bible includes many verses about encouragement. Look up the verses below and note what additional information is given about encouragement.

- Ephesians 4:29

- Hebrews 10:24–25

- Jude 1:20

DEEPER EXPERIENCE

> "With this sublime prayer-wish, the historical and personal portion of the epistle comes to a close. If Timothy's report had contained no account of 'what is lacking in your faith' (v. 10) the letter might suitably have closed here. But the mention of the deficiencies in the faith of the readers prepares the way for the second half of the letter, which deals with the needed instructions and exhortations." (D. Edmond Hiebert, *1 & 2 Thessalonians*, p. 168)

CONSIDER

Consider the circular path of encouragement in verses 1–13. Describe where it began and how it spread to impact others in this chapter.

_____

_____

_____

_____

ACTING ON GOD'S WORD

Our faith in God was never meant to be lived in isolation. The enemy loves to make us feel alone and does what he can to make us think we are abandoned and isolated. God created relationships. The most important one is with Him. But He also put people all around us so that other relationships can be developed by offering Christ-centered encouragement and support. As we saw in 1 Thessalonians 3, when there is a faith bond in a relationship, the relationship takes on new meaning. Not only is it one of love, but also one of a mutual trust in God where faith can be established, and lives are encouraged as each person cares for the other.

1. Identify a relationship where, like Paul, you have helped establish someone's faith as well as encouraged them in their Christian walk. Share some specifics about this relationship and how God has used you in this person's life.

2. Identify a relationship where someone has been like Paul to you. Share how this person helped build up your faith in God while also encouraging you in Christ.

3. Paul pointed out two ways a person's faith can be rocked or challenged. Going back to our example of ballast, the ballast (faith) works hardest when a wave comes. How have you seen your faith tested recently? Has your faith kept you steady when that wave came? Explain.

   a. As you worked through this lesson, is there anything you learned about establishing a deeper faith in God that God is calling you to apply to your life? If so, what? How will you go about working in this area?

4. 1 Thessalonians 3 ends with a prayer for the Thessalonian believers. Paul was not only just a man of faith but was also one of prayer. His faith acted in many tangible ways as he was burdened to share the gospel with others and would proceed to "walk" with them. When he couldn't be there in person, he wrote letters. End this week by being an encouragement in a similar way to the people you identified above. Pray for them, write a letter, send an email or text, or call the person who has most influenced your faith and thank them. Ask them how you can be praying for them. Then do the same for the person you have come alongside.

DELIGHTING IN GOD'S WORD

GET CAUGHT UP IN SCRIPTURE

Read Week 4's memory verses from the cards you cut apart from the back of your workbook. Next, write the verses below to encourage your memorization of them, and then place the card somewhere you will see it throughout the week.

1 Thessalonians 3:12–13

Try to memorize the verses on all eight memory cards by the time you finish the study.

Close in Prayer

WEEK 4: CAUGHT UP IN A FAITH-FILLED LIFE

Teaching Title _____

Teaching Videos and handouts are available for free at www.delightinginthelord.com.

WEEK 4: CAUGHT UP IN A FAITH-FILLED LIFE

Teaching Title _____

Teaching Videos and handouts are available for free at www.delightinginthelord.com.

WEEK 5

CAUGHT UP WITH AN ETERNAL PERSPECTIVE

In the short time Paul was with the Thessalonian believers, he instructed them in the basic matters of godly living while also giving them an eternal perspective. The choices they made each day would impact eternity. How they lived mattered. Before placing their faith in Jesus Christ, everything they did was to please themselves. Societal norms and standards were theirs. If everyone did it, it must be acceptable. But now, as children of God, their focus should be on Jesus and living for Him. The word of the Lord became their guide and the Holy Spirit their empowerment. But their obedience would be required as they cooperated with God's sanctifying work in each of them. Paul wrote to them in 1 Thessalonians 4 to encourage them to keep growing in the holiness of the Lord.

With the backdrop of holy living, Paul also taught them about the eternal kingdom of God. They would enter God's eternal kingdom when they died. It seemed for them, like us, that this reality was distant, far away, and maybe even hard to understand. Questions swirled in their heads. Paul urged them to live as though this future truth could happen tomorrow. It needed to be brought into clear focus and have an impact on their present lifestyle and heart motivations.

ARE YOU LIVING IN SUCH A WAY THAT WHEN JESUS RETURNS YOU ARE READY?

You'll see in this chapter Paul uses the pronoun "we" when talking about the Lord's return. He thought he'd be alive to witness Christ's return. He lived his life as if that day was close. We should live the same way. One day soon, Jesus will return in the clouds to bring His children home to God. The Lord will descend from heaven with a shout, an angel heralding His entry, and the trumpet of God sounding forth. Upon hearing the Father's voice, the dead will rise, and then those living will join Jesus in the air. Can you only imagine that moment?

If you've ever sat in the nosebleed section of a sports stadium or tried to bring something far away into focus, you understand the benefit of binoculars. Once you bring the binoculars to your eyes, the distance becomes clear. The obscure players on the field look like they are right in front of you. It's as if Paul is telling us all to live each day using binoculars.

Jesus' imminent return should impact the way we live. Are you living in such a way that when Jesus returns you are ready? Lord, never let us lose sight of You. May these verses in 1 Thessalonians 4 remind us to live in a way that honors God today as we eagerly seek His return in the not-so-distant tomorrow.

We have some meaty, spiritual topics to cover in these verses. Please set aside a bit more time this week to finish this lesson.

Open in Prayer

Prepare your heart before studying by filling in the prayer prompts and praying them back to the Lord as you begin.

God, You are…

God, forgive me for…

God, thank You for…

God, please help me…

Receiving God's Word

Read 1 Thessalonians 4

Experiencing God's Word

Instructions on how to live a life that pleases God (4:1-12) → Christ's return for His church (4:13-18)

EXPERIENCE 1 (15 minutes)

OBSERVATION OF 1 THESSALONIANS 4:1–18

Following are verse-by-verse questions to help you get a broad understanding of the chapter. The answers will be found directly in the text.

1. Read 1 Thessalonians 4:1–2. What does Paul urge the young church to continue doing?

2. Read 1 Thessalonians 4:3–7. What is the will of God for those who know God?

3. How does Paul describe the person in verse 5 who doesn't know God? What is this person ruled by?

4. What truth do you learn about mankind and God in verse 8?

5. Once again Paul encourages the Thessalonians. What are they doing well according to verses 9 and 10?

6. Read 1 Thessalonians 4:11–12. List the advice Paul gives to the believers and the effect it will have on their lives and those around them.

7. Paul is concerned with the ignorance of the Thessalonians in verses 13–14. What was his concern?

8. What good news do we learn about in verses 15–17? Describe this event.

9. According to 1 Thessalonians 4:18, what should the Thessalonians do with the truths Paul just shared with them in the preceding verses?

> ### CONSIDER
> Consider how Paul ends 1 Thessalonians 4. Why would his words found at the end of this chapter be comforting?
>
> _____
>
> _____
>
> _____

EXPERIENCE 2 (25 minutes)

LIVING A SANCTIFIED LIFE
1 Thessalonians 4:1–12

There is a significant shift between chapters three and four of 1 Thessalonians. Up until this point, Paul has primarily been writing about his previous visit and commending them about their work of faith, their labor of love, and their perseverance in hope. However, you may have noticed in the last verse of chapter three, Paul's concluding prayer transitioned into the content of chapter four. He wrote, "[may the Lord] establish your hearts blameless in holiness before our God and Father at the coming of our Lord Jesus Christ with all His saints." This verse captures the two main themes found in chapter four—sanctification and Christ's return. The first one we'll look at is the Holy Spirit's work of sanctification.

1. Read 1 Thessalonians 4:1–2 and 1 Thessalonians 2:13. Paul is urging the Thessalonians to live in a way that pleases God. What did Paul say he used as the standard for the commands he had given them?

2. Pleasing God is not just an outward work. It should start in the heart and show itself through our choices. Obedience will always be required. Read 1 Corinthians 6:19–20. What truth does Paul share that should motivate a believer's choices and why?

DEEPER EXPERIENCE

"As a guiding principle of Christian behavior, 'pleasing God' is a radical concept. It strikes at the roots of our discipleship and challenges the reality of our profession. How can we claim to know and love God if we do not seek to please Him?" (John Stott, 1 & 2 Thessalonians: Living in the End Times, p.21)

3. Read 1 Thessalonians 4:3a. In this verse we learn that it is God's will for every believer in Jesus Christ to be sanctified. In all simplicity, something that is sanctified in Christ is set apart for God's glory and purposes. When we place our trust in Jesus, accepting Christ's payment on the cross for our sins, God forgives us for all our sins. In theological terms, we are justified or vindicated of our sins, forgiven, and cleansed through Jesus' righteousness. In this moment of our salvation, we are both justified and sanctified. We are now set apart for God—sanctified, as well as being sanctified each day. The word *sanctification* in Greek is *hagiasmos* (Strong's G38). It means to be consecrated to the Lord in holiness. The process of becoming more and more holy (or Christlike) takes a lifetime and looks different for each person. Read the following verses and note what you learn about sanctification.

   - Malachi 3:2–3

   - 2 Corinthians 3:16–18

   - Philippians 3:12

   - Colossians 3:8–10

   - 1 John 1:8–9

4. Sanctification is both an active and passive work of the Holy Spirit in the life of a believer. Obedience and surrender are needed. Read the following verses and write down how you can pursue holiness (active) and how the Holy Spirit works on your behalf (passive).

   Active (what we can do)

   - Romans 12:1–2

   - 2 Corinthians 7:1

   Passive (what the Holy Spirit does)

   - Romans 8:34

   - 1 Corinthians 6:11

   - Galatians 5:18–23

   - Hebrews 12:2

5. Paul addresses sexual immorality in 1 Thessalonians 4:3–7. In the Greek culture of Paul's day, there was wide approval given for all forms of sexual indulgences. In 1 Thessalonians 4:4 Paul instructs the Thessalonians to "know how to possess his own vessel in sanctification and honor." Based on what you just learned in question 4, what did Paul mean by saying this? What is a believer's responsibility regarding sexual purity/immorality?

6. Read the following verses to better understand Paul's strong instruction on honoring God with our bodies.

   - Matthew 5:27–28

   - 1 Corinthians 6:9–10,18

   - 1 Corinthians 7:2–3

   - Hebrews 13:4

DEEPER EXPERIENCE

> "The idea that any kind of extramarital sex was wrong was quite foreign to the Greek mind. A blatant double standard existed. Wives were expected to be chaste, mothers of children, and keepers at home. Married men, however, could do as they pleased. They could keep mistresses and concubines and frequent prostitutes with full approval of society. Conventional morality saw nothing wrong in having affairs, committing sodomy, or indulging in premarital and extramarital sex. Our own social norms, indeed, are fast degenerating into those of ancient Greece. Paul's warnings against immorality are as needful today as they were in his day, and they sound as strange to our contemporaries as they did to his early Greek converts." (John Phillips, Exploring 1 & 2 Thessalonians, p.100)

7. Read 1 Thessalonians 4:8. Explain what Paul meant when he wrote that those who do not receive his teachings on personal holiness "does not reject man but God."

8. Paul commends the Thessalonians in verses 9–10 for loving their brothers and sisters in Christ well. Two forms of love are expressed in these verses, phileo love (brotherly love) and agape love (selfless love). How are they fulfilling the commandment Jesus gave in John 13:34–35?

9. Read 1 Thessalonians 4:11–12. How do verses 11–12 tie together with verses 9–10 and the sanctifying work of God in a believer's life?

DEEPER EXPERIENCE

"As we review this section, we see how practical the Christian walk really is. The obedient Christian will have a holy life by abstaining from sexual sin; a harmonious life by loving the brethren; and an honest life by working with his hands and not meddling in the affairs of others. When unsaved people see Christ magnified in this kind of a life, they will either oppose it with envy or desire to have it for themselves. Either way, God is glorified." (Warren Wiersbe, Be Ready: Living in Light of Christ's Return, p. 87)

CONSIDER

Paul expresses his desire for the Thessalonians' walk with God to increase ("more and more," and "lack nothing"). Consider how the process of sanctification accomplishes Paul's desire in the life of a believer. Write your thoughts below.

EXPERIENCE 3 (25 minutes)

LIVING WITH ETERNITY IN FOCUS
1 Thessalonians 4:13–18

After urging the Thessalonian believers to live a sanctified life, Paul addresses the reason why; Christ is returning at any moment to take His church home to be with Him. It is assumed that while Paul was with the Thessalonians, he had taught them about Christ's return. As time passed, loved ones who trusted in Jesus as their Savior had died. The Thessalonians were concerned that their recently deceased brothers and sisters in Christ would miss out on receiving the resurrected life with Christ that Paul had told them about. What would their eternity look like? Would they ever see their loved ones again? Grieved by this prospect, Paul comforts them with the hope we have in Jesus. Jesus is coming, and at His return, believers, both dead and alive, will spend eternity with Him. This hope is for all believers.

1. In 1 Thessalonians 4:13–15 Paul uses the words "fallen asleep" (v. 13), "sleep in Jesus" (v. 14), and "asleep" (v. 15). Read Matthew 27:51–53 and Daniel 12:1–2. What does sleep refer to in these verses?

2. Paul tells us in 1 Thessalonians 5:23 that we all have a physical body, a soul (the inner person/personality), and a spirit (that which enables us to communicate with God). The spirit part of human beings sets us apart from the animal kingdom as animals possess just a body and soul. Read 2 Corinthians 5:1–8. Describe what happens to the physical body, soul, and spirit when a person of faith dies.

   a. How is sleep a good spiritual metaphor in 1 Thessalonians 4:13–15?

3. Read 1 Thessalonians 4:14. From this verse, describe the difference between those who "sleep" and those who "sleep in Jesus."

4. Paul gives a spiritual truth in verse 14 regarding those alive and those who have previously died in faith. He says in verse 14 that God will bring with Him those who sleep in Jesus. To further understand what Paul is saying, read 1 Corinthians 15:3–8 and 12–23 and answer the following questions:

   a. What fact does Paul share about Jesus and what authenticates this fact? (vs. 3–8; 12)

   b. What question does Paul address and how is Jesus' example the basis for our faith? (vs. 12–16)

   c. What effect does the truth of Jesus' death and resurrection have on our life and death? (vs. 17–19)

   d. Explain how Christ is the firstfruit of those who have fallen asleep.

74 | CAUGHT UP

5. How do the verses in 1 Corinthians help you understand the phrase in Thessalonians 4 when Paul says, "lest you sorrow as others who have no hope"? Explain the difference between sorrow with hope in death and sorrow without hope in death.

   a. Read 2 Peter 3:9 and Luke 23:39–43. How do these verses offer encouragement regarding the salvation of loved ones, death, and God's heart?

DEEPER EXPERIENCE

> "Those who fall asleep are Christians who die. The figure of sleep for death is common in the New Testament (cf. Mark 5:39; John 11:11). This is not sleep of the soul, however, because Paul wrote elsewhere that a Christian who is absent from his body is present with the Lord (2 Corinthians 5:8; cf. Phil 1:23; 1 Thess. 5:10). It is rather the 'sleep' of the body in the earth until it is resurrected, changed into a glorious body, and reunited with the soul (1 Cor. 15:35–57; 2 Cor. 5:1–9)." (John F. Walvoord and Roy B. Zuck, The Bible Knowledge Commentary, p. 703).

6. Read 1 Thessalonians 4:15–17 and 1 Corinthians 15:51–54. When Christ returns, what will happen to the bodies of those who previously died? What will happen to those who are still alive at Christ's return?

7. We (Brenda and Stacy) teach from a pre-tribulation scriptural interpretation. Based on this belief, the events described in 1 Thessalonians 4:15–17 detail an event called the rapture of the church which precedes the 7-year tribulation period given in Matthew 24.

   Read the following verses in 1 Thessalonians and describe how they support a pre-tribulation interpretation of the rapture of the church. As you read the verses, consider how Paul's exhortations would be different if he was warning them of impending tribulation versus new life with Christ.

   - 1 Thessalonians 1:10

   - 1 Thessalonians 4:13–18

   - 1 Thessalonians 5:9–10

   - 2 Thessalonians 1:3–10

DEEPER EXPERIENCE

"This passage [1 Thessalonians 4:14–17] is the basis for the New Testament doctrine of the rapture, the catching away of believers to be with Jesus. The word rapture is not in the ancient Greek text, but comes from the Latin Vulgate, which translates the phrase caught up with rapturus, from which we get our English word rapture." (David Guzik, Enduring Word, www.blueletterbible.org)

DEEPER EXPERIENCE

"The Jewish people were familiar with trumpets, because trumpets were used to declare war, to announce special times and seasons, and to gather the people for a journey (see Numbers 10). In the Roman Empire, trumpets were used to announce the arrival of a great person. When God gave the Law to Israel, the event was preceded by a trumpet blast (Exodus 19:18–20)." (Warren Wiersbe, The Bible Exposition Commentary: New Testament Vol. 2, p. 180)

8. The phrase *caught up* in Greek is *harpazō* (Strong's G726). The Greek meaning of this word and its roots add another layer to our understanding of what will happen when Jesus returns for His church. Look at the meanings of the phrase *caught up* below and the verses next to the definitions. Explain how this adds to your understanding of God's heart when He returns.

- "Eagerly claim for one's own self" (Isaiah 43:1)

- "To snatch out or away by force" (1 Thessalonians 4:17)

- "To move from its place" (John 14:1–3)

9. 1 Thessalonians 4:18 ends by telling us to comfort one another with the truth Paul just shared. How are these realities regarding Christ's return a cause for faith and hope as well as comfort for us to share with others?

CONSIDER

Consider what Paul said in 1 Thessalonians 1:3 as he commended them for their persevering hope. How do these verses strengthen their hope in God while they wait for Christ's return?

_____
_____
_____
_____

Acting on God's Word

Paul has encouraged us in many ways in this chapter. In the first part of the chapter, he urges us to live a life that is holy and pleasing to God. As we pursue a sanctified lifestyle, we maintain a good testimony to others who have not yet accepted the gospel for themselves. By living in this manner, Christ is magnified in our lives, and hopefully, others will be drawn to Jesus because of His testimony seen in us. Our lives should look different than those who don't know Jesus as their Lord and Savior.

In the latter part of the chapter, Paul encourages the Thessalonians regarding the return of Jesus. This is referred to by Christians as the rapture. Those who have already died after putting their faith in God will be caught up first and then the living Christians will join them in the air.

> PAUL ENCOURAGED THE THESSALONIANS NOT ONLY REGARDING THEIR SANCTIFICATION BUT ALSO THE COMING OF JESUS.

Paul encouraged the Thessalonians not only regarding their sanctification but also the coming of Jesus. It may seem strange that Paul joined these encouragements together. Yet, God uses His people to draw others to the saving knowledge of Christ so they, too, will be caught up in the air at Jesus' return. We can rest knowing that one day Jesus will finally return. When He does, His sanctifying work in us will be complete and we will see Him face to face entering the eternal joy of the Lord. That future reality should encourage us in the way we live our lives today.

1. What does "being caught up with an eternal perspective" mean to you?

2. If you struggle living each day with an eternal perspective, what specifically hinders you from living in the spiritual reality of Christ's return?

3. How does or doesn't your life demonstrate that you are looking forward to the day Christ returns? When you consider the moment of His return, what thoughts or emotions come to your heart?

4. The sanctifying work of the Holy Spirit is ongoing in the life of a believer. How have you seen this sanctifying work in your life? How has God changed you since you put your faith in Jesus?

5. How is the Lord sanctifying you right now? What areas of your life has He been working on that require your obedience and surrendering to Him?

DELIGHTING IN GOD'S WORD

GET CAUGHT UP IN SCRIPTURE

Read Week 5's memory verses from the cards you cut apart from the back of your workbook. Next, write the verses below to encourage your memorization of them, and then place the card somewhere you will see it throughout the week.

1 Thessalonians 4:16-17

Try to memorize the verses on all eight memory cards by the time you finish the study.

Close in Prayer

WEEK 5: CAUGHT UP WITH AN ETERNAL PERSPECTIVE

Teaching Title _____

Teaching Videos and handouts are available for free at www.delightinginthelord.com.

WEEK 5: CAUGHT UP WITH AN ETERNAL PERSPECTIVE

Teaching Title _____

Teaching Videos and handouts are available for free at www.delightinginthelord.com.

WEEK 6

CAUGHT UP IN GOD'S WILL

Jesus had much to teach His disciples during his three short years of ministry. Sometimes He taught them in large, public crowds, and other times He instructed them in private, intimate settings. In Luke 11, after Jesus concluded praying, one of the disciples asked Him to teach them how to pray. Jesus responded with what has become the most well-known prayer in the Bible. He said,

"Our Father in heaven,
Hallowed be Your name.
<u>Your kingdom come.</u>
<u>Your will be done</u>
On earth as it is in heaven.
Give us this day our daily bread.
And forgive us our debts,
As we also forgive our debtors.
And do not lead us into temptation,
But deliver us from the evil one.
For Yours is the kingdom and the power and the glory forever. Amen."
Matthew 6:9b–13

> PAUL WANTED THEM TO BE READY FOR CHRIST'S KINGDOM TO COME AND SEE GOD'S WILL BE DONE WHILE THEY WAITED.

Over the centuries this prayer has been repeated both corporately by countless congregations and privately by an unknown number of individuals. These verses are short and succinct yet contain truths we will find Paul echoing in his final chapter of 1 Thessalonians. Paul wanted them to be ready for <u>Christ's kingdom to come</u> and see God's <u>will be done</u> while they waited.

The Thessalonians had an individual responsibility to be watchful and sober and to live in a way that reflected God. Their life should have demonstrated a healthy spiritual life that could be seen walking in the light. They did not have to fear the future kingdom to come because they were standing before God. They needed to understand that on the day He returns, they would not be appointed to wrath but instead had salvation through Jesus Christ. They should comfort each other with this truth until that day.

The Thessalonians also had a collective responsibility as a church to do the will of God. Paul gave them instructions on how to interact with the leadership and each other and how to behave orderly in corporate worship. Once he finished his last bit of instruction, he closed with a prayer for the young church. His prayer, like Jesus' famous one in Luke 11, entreats God to minister to a believer's spirit, soul, and body.

As you prepare to study 1 Thessalonians chapter 5, reread the Lord's prayer. Pray each line back to Jesus, the One who prayed it to His Father first. May we be expectant of His kingdom coming and, in the meantime, His will being done through us on earth as it is in heaven.

Open in Prayer

Prepare your heart before studying by filling in the prayer prompts and praying them back to the Lord as you begin.

God, You are…

God, forgive me for…

God, thank You for…

God, please help me…

RECEIVING GOD'S WORD

Read 1 Thessalonians 5

EXPERIENCING GOD'S WORD

| The return of Christ and its impact on believers and non-believers (5:1-11) | How to interact with church leadership (5:12-13) | How to care for other believers (5:14-15) | Christian community (5:16-22) | Paul's closing prayer (5:23-28) |

EXPERIENCE 1 (10 minutes)

OBSERVATION OF 1 THESSALONIANS 5:1–28

Below are verse-by-verse questions to help you get a broad understanding of the chapter. The answers will be found directly in the text.

1. What analogies does Paul give in 1 Thessalonians 5:1–4 for the Lord's return?

2. Who is the "they" Paul is referring to in verses 1–3? How does he contrast this group of people with his readers in verse 5?

3. Paul makes another contrast in verses 6–8 by using the analogies of sleep and drunkenness. What is he saying?

4. In verse 8b Paul gives instructions to his readers on how they should live. He brings back the topics of faith, love, and hope that were introduced in 1 Thessalonians 1. How are these attributes now protective? What is required regarding these?

5. What reasons does Paul give in verses 9–10 about why we should live awake and sober?

6. Use verses 11–15 to explain how believers should behave as they live in a diverse community.

7. What is the will of God for every believer according to verses 16–18?

8. Paul gives a list of commands in verses 19–22. These commands center around both individual and corporate responsibilities as a believer. What does Paul say not to do? What does Paul say to do?

9. How do verses 23–24 remind us that we aren't expected to live our spiritual lives without help? How do these verses relieve the pressure of perfection?

10. How does Paul end 1 Thessalonians in verses 25–28?

CONSIDER

After examining 1 Thessalonians 5, consider why Paul would combine truths of the Lord's return with warnings and commands for the believer in Christ. Write your thoughts below.

_____
_____
_____
_____

EXPERIENCE 2 (20 minutes)

THY KINGDOM COME
1 Thessalonians 5:1–11

Having ended 1 Thessalonians 4 with spiritual truths regarding the rapture, Paul now addresses the effect the rapture should have on believers while still living and waiting. After Christ's return for the church, a series of events will unfold in Jesus' second coming to earth. Matthew 24 and the book of Revelation detail these events otherwise known as the Tribulation and Great Tribulation. Saying, "You have no need that I should write to you," Paul didn't need to inform the Thessalonians of these specific details about the timing (1 Thess. 5:1). They had already received instruction about this from him when he was in Thessalonica.

Having addressed the rapture, Paul turns his attention toward God's second coming, when He will establish His eternal kingdom on earth. The Lord's prayer comes to mind as we study these verses when Jesus said, "Thy kingdom come, thy will be done on earth as it is in heaven" (Matthew 6:10). The Lord's purposes will prevail above all. One day all things will be made new (Revelation 21:5). There will be a new heaven and a new earth. The old will pass away, and God will dwell with His redeemed people forever (Revelation 21:3). This future time will be a time of judgment for those who have rejected Jesus. Paul concludes his first letter to the young believers in Thessalonica here. He doesn't go into the details of Christ's second coming but affirms the truth of the event and how we should live while waiting. He encourages them to look forward to His kingdom coming.

> THE OLD WILL PASS AWAY, AND GOD WILL DWELL WITH HIS REDEEMED PEOPLE FOREVER.

1. Read 1 Thessalonians 5:1–4. Paul now addresses the "day of the Lord" (v. 2). What details were pressing on the hearts and minds of the Thessalonian believers regarding this day? What had Paul already instructed them about this future time?

2. Paul uses the phrase, "the day of the Lord" in verse 2. Look up the following verses and note what you learn about this day.

- Amos 5:18–20

- Joel 2:1–3

- Matthew 24:21–24; 29–30

- Acts 2:17–21

DEEPER EXPERIENCE

"The day of the Lord is a future period of time in which God will be at work in world affairs more directly and dramatically than He has been since the earthly ministry of the Lord Jesus Christ. It is a time referred to by many Old Testament prophets (e.g., Isaiah 13:9–11; Joel 2:28–32; Zeph.1:14–18, 3:14–15). As these and other Old Testament verses indicate, the day of the Lord will include both judgment and blessing. That day begins immediately after the Rapture of the church and ends with the Millennium. This day is a major theme of prophecy with its fullest exposition in Revelation 6–19." (John F. Walvoord, Roy B. Zuck, The Bible Knowledge Commentary, p. 705)

3. After looking up the verses in question 2, think of the analogies Paul gives in 1 Thessalonians 5:2–3 for the day of the Lord. Explain why these are good analogies that describe the second coming of Jesus. Read the verses that accompany the analogies below for more context.

- Thief in the night
  (Matthew 24:36–44)

- Pregnancy
  (Matthew 24:4–13)

DEEPER EXPERIENCE

> "The impenitent and wicked world will be sunk in carnal security when he [the Lord] comes. They will regard themselves as safe. They will see no danger. They will give no heed to warning. They will be unprepared for his advent. So it has always been. It seems to be universal truth in regard to all the visitations of God to wicked men for punishment, that he comes upon them at a time when they are not expecting him, and that they have no faith in the predictions of his advent. So it was in the time of the flood; in the destruction of Sodom, Gomorrah, and Jerusalem; in the overthrow of Babylon; so it is when the sinner dies, and so it will be when the Lord Jesus shall return to judge the world." (Albert Barnes, Barnes' Notes on the New Testament: Ephesians to Philemon, p. 52–53)

4. In 1 Thessalonians 5:3–9 Paul makes a distinction between believers and non-believers by using the pronouns "they" and "us." He uses darkness and night as well as light and day to emphasize this contrast. Read Romans 1:18–25; 29–31. How does Paul describe both the person and works of darkness?

a. According to Romans 1:18, how must a righteous God respond to such a person and these works of darkness? How does this tie into what Paul is saying about Christ's second coming?

5. It can be hard to reconcile the love of God with the judgment of God seen in 1 Thessalonians 5. Remember what you learned in Week 5, question 5a of Experience 3 about God's heart for all men. Read Romans 2:2–11. What do you learn about God's heart, man's heart, and God's judgment?

6. 1 Thessalonians 5:4 begins with the words, "But you, brethren" to distinguish the believers from the non-believers. Paul reminds the Thessalonian believers of their identity in Christ as well as their responsibility before Him in verses 4–10. According to these verses, what does Paul need them to remember concerning their identity and responsibility?

a. Paul said something similar in Ephesians 5:8–18. How does Paul's message in Ephesians support and add to his message in 1 Thessalonians 5?

7. In 1 Thessalonians 5:6–8 Paul tells us how believers can protect themselves from falling into spiritual lethargy and a lifestyle defined by darkness. The Greek word used for *sleep* in verse 6 is a different word than the one used for sleep in 1 Thessalonians 4:14. It is *katheudō* (Strong's G2518). It means to yield to sloth and sin; be indifferent to your salvation. What are Paul's instructions? Describe how they offer spiritual protection.

DEEPER EXPERIENCE

> "For those of us who are saved and who are expecting and waiting for the Lord's return, it is comforting to know that we will have no part in the woes of this world during the great tribulation. We will be with the Lord in the Father's house. When He descends to the earth to set up His kingdom, we will come with Him and reign with Him." (H.A. Ironside, *1 & 2 Thessalonians: Ironside Commentaries*, p. 51)

8. How do verses 9–10 offer hope and encouragement for believers? Why would Paul tell us in verse 11 to comfort and lift each other up with these truths as we wait for Christ's return?

CONSIDER

Consider that every chapter of 1 Thessalonians 1–4 ends with a reference to the coming of the Lord Jesus Christ. In 1 Thessalonians 5 Paul devotes 11 verses to this topic as well. Paul was deliberate to point out the Thessalonians' identity in Christ (children of the day, light, Christ) and their responsibilities. Consider why our identity in Christ and the responsibilities therein are important regarding the coming of the Lord and write your thoughts below.

_____

_____

_____

_____

EXPERIENCE 3 (25 minutes)

THY WILL BE DONE
1 Thessalonians 5:12–28

In the preceding 11 verses of this chapter, Paul reminded the Thessalonians about their identity in Christ as children of the light and the importance of that identity as they waited for Christ's return and ultimately God's eternal kingdom. As Paul reminded them of the swift judgment coming to those who have rejected Jesus as their Savior, his main concern centered around their lifestyle as they waited. As hard as it was to hear of God's coming judgment, they were saved and being sanctified.

Because of their standing in Christ, the Thessalonians had a responsibility before God to live their lives according to His will. Paul begins verse 12 by addressing the way a believer in Christ should live while they await His return. Every believer should be actively pursuing God's will for their life and living in a way that demonstrates their commitment and love for Him.

EVERY BELIEVER SHOULD BE ACTIVELY PURSUING GOD'S WILL FOR THEIR LIFE AND LIVING IN A WAY THAT DEMONSTRATES THEIR COMMITMENT AND LOVE FOR HIM.

As you read these verses, it might be easy to conclude that Paul created a long list of do's and don'ts to be followed. However, consider the deeper intent Paul likely had for his readers. Paul wrote in 1 Thessalonians 4:3, "For this is the will of God, your sanctification: that you should abstain from sexual immorality." When God purifies our lives, he adds more of Himself to the areas He sanctifies. In doing so, our actions change individually which impact the church.

As you complete Experience 3, you will find that Paul divides his thoughts into three topics that pertain to interacting with others in the church. Verses 12–13 cover how to engage with the church leadership, while verses 14–15 cover how to care for other believers, and finally, in verses 16–24 Paul addresses how to please God in a corporate worship setting. You will quickly notice Paul reiterates what he has already taught them throughout the letter. There will be questions that incorporate this repetition.

---

1. Read 1 Thessalonians 5:12–13 in the NKJV and fill in the missing blanks from the verse.

   And we urge you, brethren, to _____ those who _____ among you,

   and are _____ and admonish you, and to _____

   _____ for their work's sake. Be at _____ among yourselves.

a. Why would Paul urge the Thessalonians to recognize and esteem the church leaders as well as live peacefully as the body of Christ? Keep in mind what Paul shared with them in verses 1–11. What does this suggest may be happening among them?

2. Go back and read 1 Thessalonians 2:9–11 and 4:9. How was Paul's leadership a godly example for them to follow especially with the issues the church in Thessalonica is facing?

DEEPER EXPERIENCE

> "If a Christian can't esteem and love their pastor, they should either get on their knees, asking the Holy Spirit to change their heart, or go somewhere else and put themselves under a pastor they do esteem and love." (David Guzik, www.blueletterbible.org)

3. Paul now moves from interactions with the leadership to how to treat other believers who require special attention. Read 1 Thessalonians 5:14. Based on the NKJV of this verse, match the following pieces of the commands together.

ACTION:	TO WHOM:
Warn	the weak
Comfort	with all
Uphold	the unruly
Be patient	the fainthearted

a. The word *idle/disruptive* (NIV) has been substituted for the word *unruly* (NKJV) in 1 Thessalonians 5:14. What did Paul previously recommend in 1 Thessalonians 4:11 for this kind of problem?

WEEK 6: CAUGHT UP IN GOD'S WILL | 93

b. The word *disheartened* (NIV) has been substituted for the word *fainthearted* in 1 Thessalonians 5:14. What did Paul warn might happen in 1 Thessalonians 3:3 to cause them to be disheartened?

4. Read 1 Thessalonians 5:15 and Matthew 5:43–48. What command does Paul repeat from Jesus' teachings that when obeyed would affect both individuals and the body of Christ?

a. Read 1 Corinthians 1:10 and John 17:20-23. According to these verses, how is Paul's exhortations to the Thessalonian church in 1 Thessalonians 5:12-15 upholding God's will?

5. Read 1 Thessalonians 5:16–18. Paul tells us that there are three more things that are God's will for us. We are to rejoice, pray, and give thanks. Read the following verses found in 1 Thessalonians and write down what Paul already taught on these three topics. Be sure to note the truths/personal example that encourages rejoicing, prayer, and thanksgiving.

- Rejoice: 1 Thessalonians 1:6, 4:13–18

- Pray: 1 Thessalonians 1:2, 3:11–13, 5:25

- Thanksgiving: 1 Thessalonians 1:2, 2:13

6. 1 Thessalonians 5:16–18 is God's will for our lives, but it can be difficult to do! Read Paul's similar words of encouragement in Philippians 4:4–7, 13. What is the same between these two sets of verses and what is different?

a. Based on the verses in Philippians, how are we empowered to do God's will?

7. Read 1 Thessalonians 5:19–22. In this portion of Scripture, Paul focuses on how to receive guidance from God so His will can be done. Below are the commands Paul gives. Read the verses that accompany the commands and note what you learn.

   a. Do not quench the Spirit:
   - Ephesians 4:29–32

   - 1 John 4:1–6

   b. Abstain from every form of evil:
   - Mark 7:20–23

DEEPER EXPERIENCE

> "We can quench the fire of the Holy Spirit by our doubt, our indifference, our rejection of Him, or by the distraction of others. When people start to draw attention to themselves, it is a sure quench to the Spirit." (David Guzik, www.blueletterbible.org)

8. Read 1 Thessalonians 5:23–28. This is Paul's closing prayer for the Thessalonians. He begins the prayer with the personal sanctification of the believers. How is our sanctification tied to the return of Christ?

a. What truth about God is found in verse 24?

CONSIDER

Consider God's will as stated in 1 Thessalonians 4:3, 5:9–10, and 16–19. God's heart is seen through His will for all of us. What have you learned about God's will for mankind and the importance of our response/cooperation?

_____

_____

_____

_____

ACTING ON GOD'S WORD

When we consider the will of God, it is easy to get overwhelmed by the enormity of the subject. Do you find yourself praying for God's will in your life and find your prayer wrapped around a specific circumstance or outcome? Lord, is it your will for me to….and you fill in the blank. Most of us want so desperately to be living in the will of God for our lives. It is a good focus for sure!

But Paul made it simple in his letter to the Thessalonians by culminating his encouragement in chapter 5 about the will of God. God's will is interlocked with His character and plans. He desires for all of us to be in a relationship with Him through Jesus and desires to live with us forever (1 Thess. 5:9–10). From beginning to end, He works more of Himself into our lives as He sanctifies us, so on that day when He either calls us home or returns to get us, we are preserved blameless at His coming (1 Thess. 5:23–24). It is often through our life circumstances that God accomplishes His will in each of us.

> GOD'S WILL IS INTERLOCKED WITH HIS CHARACTER AND PLANS.

God is faithful to do His sanctifying work in and through us so that others will come to know Him too. Our cooperation allows room for God to accomplish His will in us. God's will is not so much about the specific circumstances of our lives but more about the character of Christ in us as we live each day preparing for His return.

Paul said it this way in Colossians 1:27, "To them God willed to make known what are the riches of the glory of this mystery among the Gentiles: which is Christ in you, the hope of glory." Let's take what Paul said to the Thessalonians and apply it now to our own lives.

1. Is there an area of your life where you are asking for God's will to be made known? Fill in the blank:

   Lord, please make known your will regarding_____
   _____.

2. List all the truths you know about the Lord that will remind you of His faithfulness in the area of concern you listed above.

3. Paul reminded the Thessalonian believers of their identity in Christ (1 Thess. 5:4–10). How does your identity in Christ help you persevere as you wait on Him to make His will known in your life?

4. How is the Lord sanctifying your spirit, soul, and body as you wait on Him?

a. Are you allowing the Spirit to work in you so that God's will can be accomplished? Are you asleep spiritually or wide awake (watchful and sober)? Explain.

5. How does the truth that Jesus is returning in judgment (second coming of Christ) affect your understanding of God's will for your life?

Delighting in God's Word

GET CAUGHT UP IN SCRIPTURE

Read Week 6's memory verses from the cards you cut apart from the back of your workbook. Next, write the verses below to encourage your memorization of them, and then place the card somewhere you will see it throughout the week.

1 Thessalonians 5:23–24

Try to memorize the verses on all eight memory cards by the time you finish the study.

Close in Prayer

WEEK 6: CAUGHT UP IN GOD'S WILL

Teaching Title _____

Teaching Videos and handouts are available for free at www.delightinginthelord.com.

WEEK 6: CAUGHT UP IN GOD'S WILL

Teaching Title _____

Teaching Videos and handouts are available for free at www.delightinginthelord.com.

WEEK 7

DON'T GET CAUGHT UP IN YOUR CIRCUMSTANCES

It seems only a few months had passed before Paul felt compelled to reach back out to the young Thessalonian believers. While still in Corinth, Paul hears of the intense spiritual pressure and attacks coming against this newly formed church. Interestingly, 1 Thessalonians 1:1 and 2 Thessalonians 1:1 are the only times Paul writes to a group of people and calls them "the church." They were just that; a newly formed spiritual family held together in faith and called out from among the world to live for Jesus. Living in a cosmopolitan epicenter of sea trade and commerce brought an abundance of opportunities to evangelize. But there was also unrelenting opposition to the gospel. Deception attempted to darken the truth of the Lord's coming, and lies were being spread about Paul's teachings. It's no wonder the enemies of the gospel were trying so hard to discourage them.

> WE CAN GET CAUGHT UP IN OUR CIRCUMSTANCES, FORGETTING THAT GOD HAS A PLAN AND PURPOSE FOR OUR LIVES.

Paul heard the Thessalonians were standing strong in the Lord with the biblical undergirding shared with them. Although young in their faith, they were remaining steadfast in their faith even amid growing discouragement. Faith is often the first thing tested when trying circumstances come our way. Knowing this, Paul prayed for them (2 Thess. 1:3). What joy it must have been for him to hear his prayers were being answered. Their faith was growing, and they were also strengthening their fellow brothers and sisters in Christ. But questions swirled in their minds regarding both their oppression and their oppressors. Will this ever end? Why so much suffering? How will God intervene?

It has been said that discouragement results when disappointment is continually fed. When trials come quickly and it seems like wildfires are burning all around us, disappointment that life isn't easier can quickly turn into all-out discouragement. How easy it can be to take our eyes off Jesus and fix them on ourselves and our hardships. We can get caught up in our circumstances, forgetting that God has a plan and purpose for our lives. We must be so careful where we place our focus and attention. We either keep it on Jesus or our eyes and hearts will wander to the things of this world. Then before we know it, we become entangled in discouragement and even despair. Just like a fisherman must carefully plan where he will throw his nets, we, too, must watch where we cast our eyes and fix our hearts.

With these points in mind, Paul tenderly, but firmly, writes his second letter to the Thessalonians. With his focus on their spiritual heritage, kingdom calling, and God's ultimate glory, Paul reminds them that God will intervene one day and bring judgment to their oppressors. But just as Jesus suffered, they will too. Hatred and evil nailed Jesus to the cross and will attempt to do the same to them.

Yet, that cross became the gateway to our salvation and redemption. It was where God's judgment over sin was accomplished. Jesus' death made a way for us to live in God's freedom and forgiveness today. In Him, we can be steadfast and immovable in our faith, allowing His glory to be seen.

This chapter has a unique structure. Originally, verses 3–10 were written by Paul as one long sentence (the KJV does not have a period until the end of verse 10) with interwoven points. In examining these verses, we'll pull out two major themes while having you look at overlapping verses in the chapter.

Open in Prayer

Prepare your heart before studying by filling in the prayer prompts and praying them back to the Lord as you begin.

God, You are…

God, forgive me for…

God, thank You for…

God, please help me…

Receiving God's Word

Read 2 Thessalonians 1

Experiencing God's Word

- Paul encourages the Thessalonians in the midst of persecution (1:1-3)
- One day God will bring righteous judgment (1:4-10)
- Prayer for the Thessalonians' continued faith despite persecution (1:11-12)

EXPERIENCE 1 (10 minutes)

OBSERVATION OF 2 THESSALONIANS 1:1–12

Below are verse-by-verse questions to help you get a broad understanding of the chapter. The answers will be found directly in the text.

1. How does Paul greet the Thessalonians in 2 Thessalonians 1:1–2? You may notice that this is the same greeting he gave in 1 Thessalonians 1.

2. What does Paul acknowledge in verse 3 about the Thessalonians?

3. What was the cause of Paul's boasting when speaking of the Thessalonian believers in verse 4?

4. What is the manifest evidence of God's righteous judgment according to verses 4–5?

5. According to verses 6–8, how will God act justly and right the wrongs of their persecution?

6. Use verses 9–10 to describe how God's coming judgment confirms the choices of those persecuting the Thessalonian believers.

7. How did Paul pray for the Thessalonians in verses 11–12?

CONSIDER

Consider how the ongoing persecution could have caused the Thessalonians to get caught up in themselves and their circumstances instead of the truths of God. What might have been witnessed in their lives as a result? Consider how Paul's letter would have looked much different if this were the case.

_____

_____

_____

_____

EXPERIENCE 2 (15 minutes)

PAUL'S ENCOURAGEMENT TO ONGOING PERSECUTION
2 Thessalonians 1:3–5, 11–12

In the section below, we will cover the encouragement Paul gives the Thessalonians regarding their faith and ongoing persecution. We will examine how their faith, as exhibited in their trials, proves their salvation is genuine, and their spiritual inheritance is in heaven. As hard as their lives were, they could take comfort in their suffering because they knew God had counted them worthy of the kingdom of God.

We have broken the verses apart into two sections so that we can examine the text more closely through the lenses of difficult trials and God's intervention. In Experience 2 you will examine verses 3–5 and 11–12, and in Experience 3 you will look at verses 6–10.

1. Read 2 Thessalonians 1:3. How is Paul's gratitude for the Thessalonians in verse 3 better understood with the things he shared in 1 Thessalonians 1:1–2, and 3:5,10?

2. The Thessalonians were commended by Paul in 2 Thessalonians 1:3 for their faith and love as they endured affliction. How do faith and love work together so that the body of Christ is edified and supported through trials and difficulties? (Hebrews 10:24–25 give some suggestions for ways to do this if you need ideas.)

DEEPER EXPERIENCE

> "What were these believers enduring? Paul used several words to describe their situation: persecutions, which means 'attacks from without' or 'trials;' tribulation which literally means 'pressures' or 'afflictions that result from the trials;' and trouble (2 Thess 1:7), which means 'to be pressed into a narrow place.' No matter how we look at it, the Thessalonian Christians were not having an easy time." (Warren Wiersbe, Be Ready: Living in Light of Christ's Return, p.134)

3. Read 2 Thessalonians 1:4. Paul is boasting to other churches about the Thessalonians' patience and faith despite their persecution. The word *patience* in Greek is *hypomonē* (Strong's G5281). It means to have steadfastness, constancy, or endurance of faith in the midst of extreme suffering. Read 2 Corinthians 6:4–10. How is it possible for someone to endure trials with steadfastness?

   a. Why would Paul tell the Thessalonians that he boasts of them?

4. Read 2 Thessalonians 1:5. The words *manifest evidence* in verse 5 are found nowhere else in Scripture. This phrase means "an indication of something or a proof." Paul is saying that a person's faith and endurance in trials is "manifest evidence" that they are saved. Read Romans 3:21–26. How did God judge sin through Jesus, satisfying all of sin's consequences? How do we receive God's forgiveness for our sins while we are living on earth, thus satisfying sin's penalty?

DEEPER EXPERIENCE

> "Justification: The Greek noun for justification is derived from the Greek verb dikaioō, meaning 'to acquit' or 'to declare righteous' (used by Paul in Romans 4:2,5,5:1). It is a legal term used of a favorable verdict in a trial. The word depicts a courtroom setting, with God presiding as the Judge, determining the faithfulness of each person to the Law. In the first section of Romans, Paul makes it clear that no one can withstand God's judgment (3:9–20). The Law was not given to justify sinners but to expose their sin. To remedy this deplorable situation, God sent His Son to die for our sins, in our place. When we believe in Jesus, God imputes His righteousness to us, and we are declared righteous before God. In this way, God demonstrates that He is both a righteous Judge and the One who declares us righteous, our Justifier (3:26)." (Nelson's NKJV Study Bible, wordfocus, p. 1886)

a. What Paul is saying in 2 Thessalonians 1:5 is further reiterated in 1 Peter 1:6–9. How does our conduct in trials prove to others our spiritual standing before God?

DEEPER EXPERIENCE

> "We usually think that God is absent when we suffer, and that our suffering calls God's righteous judgment into question. Paul took the exact opposite position and insisted that the Thessalonians' suffering was evidence of the righteous judgment of God. Where suffering is coupled with righteous endurance, God's work is done. The fires of persecution and tribulation were like the purifying fires of a refiner, burning away the dross from the gold, bringing forth a pure, precious metal." (David Guzik, Enduring Word, www.blueletterbible.org)

5. Look at the second half of 2 Thessalonians 1:5 and 2 Thessalonians 1:11–12 and answer the following questions:

   a. In verses 5 and 11 the same phrase is used regarding believers. What is this phrase?

   b. Fill in the blanks from verses 5 and 11 using the New King James Version.

   - Verse 5: ...that you would be counted worthy of the _____ of _____.

   - Verse 11: ...that our God would count you worthy of this _____, and fulfill all the good _____ of His _____ and the work of _____ with _____.

   c. The word *worthy* in Greek is *axioō* (Strong's G515) and *axios* (Strong's G514). The phrase *counted worthy* is *kataxioō* (Strong's G2661). Defined together, it describes something that holds weight or has a strengthened substance. In verses 5 and 11 Paul says that the Thessalonians were "counted worthy" of the kingdom of God and His calling on their life. What does this mean?

   d. Read 2 Thessalonians 1:11–12. What is our calling and kingdom purpose?

6. Based on what you've learned, do we make ourselves worthy? Explain.

WEEK 7: DON'T GET CAUGHT UP IN YOUR CIRCUMSTANCES | 107

7. Read Philippians 1:27–29. How is this a good summary of what Paul was saying to the young church in Thessalonica even though it was written to the Philippians?

> ## CONSIDER
>
> Consider the encouragement and prayer Paul shared with the young church in Thessalonica in these verses as well as his discipleship purposes. Why do you think Paul did not pray for God to deliver them from suffering?
>
> _____
> _____
> _____
> _____

EXPERIENCE 3 (20 minutes)

GOD INTERVENES
2 Thessalonians 1:6–10

Woven throughout Paul's encouragement to the Thessalonians concerning their strong faith and endurance in hardship, we find an emphasis of God's coming judgment on their oppressors. Whereas this is a hard reality, as we don't like to think of harm coming to others, Paul explains it as part of God's just character. For believers, our judgment and penalty for sin have been paid when we place our faith in Jesus. For non-believers, their rejection of Jesus and hatred for His people will be judged by God. It will come with eternal consequences. God's destruction is coming to those who don't receive Jesus. This is God's judgment on sin.

The verses in this section are a repeat of some of the verses in Experience 2, but our hope is that you will see Paul's encouragement even though he is addressing God's coming judgment. God will intervene at the appropriate time and forever right the wrongs done against His people.

1. The NIV translation of 2 Thessalonians 1:6 says, "God is just: He will pay back trouble to those who trouble you." The NKJV says, "Since it is a righteous thing with God to repay...." The NASB says, "For after all it is only right for God to repay with affliction those who afflict you." Sometimes looking at other translations gives you a better understanding of what is being communicated. What do you learn about God in verse 6?

2. Read the following verses that speak about God's just and righteous character and note what you learn.

    - Deuteronomy 10:17–18

    - Deuteronomy 32:4

    - Psalm 33:4

    - Psalm 89:13–14

    - Isaiah 9:6–7

3. Read Psalm 51:1–6. David spoke these words to God. What did David acknowledge about himself and God's judgment?

    - David's personal acknowledgments:

    - God's judgment:

WEEK 7: DON'T GET CAUGHT UP IN YOUR CIRCUMSTANCES | 109

4. Use the NKJV to fill in the blanks below with the second half of 2 Thessalonians 1:6.

   Since it is a righteous thing with God to _____ with _____ those who _____ you.

   a. Read 2 Thessalonians 1:7–10. Skip over the first half of verse 7 for a moment. We'll come back to it shortly. Remember this is one long sentence that starts back in verse 3. What details do you learn about God's judgment of the unrighteous from verses 7–10?

   b. Read Acts 17:30–31. What do you learn about God's righteous judgment on those who reject God?

   c. Read Daniel 7:9–10 and Revelation 20:11–15. These verses describe the time of God's judgment referred to in 2 Thessalonians 1:7–10. What do you learn about this time of judgment?

5. Remember what you learned in the last lesson about those who will face God's judgment after Jesus returns in His second coming. In Experience 2, question 5 of Week 6, you looked at Romans 2:2–11. You examined the hardness of the hearts of those who rejected Jesus. Based on what you've learned, how is it a righteous thing for God to punish evil?

6. Now look at 2 Thessalonians 1:7a. What will God give to those who have endured persecution and suffering at the hand of those against the gospel?

7. Read Matthew 25:31–34 & 46. Describe the rest that God has for His children one day.

8. Jesus spoke to His disciples in Matthew 24:45–51 about the coming judgment of the Lord. How are His words both encouraging and a warning?

DEEPER EXPERIENCE

"As a reminder, Paul had written previously about the Rapture in 1 Thessalonians 4 and now in 2 Thessalonians 1 is writing about the second coming of Christ. Below is a helpful chart to explain these two chapters.

1 Thessalonians 4:13–18	2 Thessalonians 1:7–10
Christ returns in the air	Christ returns to earth
Christ comes secretly for the church	Christ comes openly with the church
Believers escape tribulation	Unbelievers experience the tribulation and judgment
Occurs at an undisclosed time	Occurs at the end of the tribulation period, the day of the Lord"

(Warren Wiersbe, Be Ready: Living in Light of Christ's Return, p. 138)

CONSIDER

Consider all that you have learned in this chapter. How would this chapter challenge the Thessalonians to not get caught up in their circumstances?

_____

_____

_____

_____

Acting on God's Word

The Thessalonians faced violent and life-threatening persecution for their faith in Christ. Those who were opposed to the gospel were tenacious and often pursued Christians from town to town looking to harm them. The aggression against the church was severe and ongoing. Therefore, Paul wrote a second letter to the Thessalonians expressing his thanks to God for their steadfast faith despite their incredible hardships.

> THOSE OF US WHO BELIEVE IN JESUS CAN RESPOND TO OUR CHALLENGING CIRCUMSTANCES DIFFERENTLY THAN THOSE WHO DO NOT KNOW CHRIST.

The Thessalonians were a source of encouragement to Paul, Silas, and Timothy. In the first chapter of his second letter, Paul included a reminder to the Thessalonians that the Lord would one day judge their perpetrators who would be held accountable for their actions. Paul concluded the chapter with a precious prayer encouraging them to continue to endure in God's power, knowing they had been counted worthy to suffer for the cause of Christ.

When we find ourselves in difficult circumstances, it isn't unusual for questions to rise up and discouragement to descend. However, how we handle these questions and discouragement matters. Those of us who believe in Jesus can respond to our challenging circumstances differently than those who do not know Christ. We can turn our eyes toward the One who knows the end from the beginning, and He will provide us with His unexplainable peace. His strength becomes ours, and it baffles the world around us.

In the United States, we do not typically face the kind of persecution the Thessalonians endured; however, having been in women's ministries for more than 15 years, we have watched God sustain ladies, as well as ourselves, through some incredibly difficult circumstances. We are often in awe of God as we listen to them share the ways God has helped them endure with hope and joy. Some of the women we know have traveled roads none of us would ever want to walk, yet their lives have spurred us on to glorify God as we stood beside them in their pain.

A witness to the faith of the Thessalonians, Paul wrote encouraging them to remain steadfast. What is the testimony of someone you know who has endured well in the face of trials and hardship? Keep that person in mind as you answer the following questions.

1. Briefly describe the set of challenging circumstances faced by the person you know. Be sure to include why it would have been so easy for the person to focus on the circumstances instead of God.

2. How did their words and actions demonstrate their faith in God and their love for others despite the hardship? Describe how their actions were a witness for God's glory.

3. When you are faced with difficult circumstances or persecution, what are your reactionary tendencies? Is there anything you can apply to your own life from witnessing this person's faith in the midst of the hardship, or from the Thessalonian's steadfast faith you observed in the text, helping you to focus more on God?

4. Do you know someone who is having a difficult time now? Write a prayer for them in the space below using 2 Thessalonians 1:11–12 as a guide. If the Lord leads you, prayerfully consider sharing your prayer with them in a text or a note to encourage them.

Delighting in God's Word

GET CAUGHT UP IN SCRIPTURE

Read Week 7's memory verse from the cards you cut apart from the back of your workbook. Next, write the verse below to encourage your memorization of the verse, and then place the card somewhere you will see it throughout the week.

2 Thessalonians 1:11

Try to memorize the verses on all eight memory cards by the time you finish the study.

Close in Prayer

WEEK 7: DON'T GET CAUGHT UP IN YOUR CIRCUMSTANCES

Teaching Title _____

Teaching Videos and handouts are available for free at www.delightinginthelord.com.

WEEK 7: DON'T GET CAUGHT UP IN YOUR CIRCUMSTANCES

Teaching Title _____

Teaching Videos and handouts are available for free at www.delightinginthelord.com.

WEEK 8

DON'T GET CAUGHT UP IN FEAR AND WORRY

As you have learned, when Paul was in Thessalonica he spent time teaching the Thessalonians about the Lord's return. He made sure to educate them on this topic as he wanted them to be prepared and ready for the glorious day to come. Once again, Paul learns of fears and worries creeping into their hearts surrounding this and other matters.

At some point between the writing of 1 and 2 Thessalonians, some commentators suggest an erroneous letter was circulated among the early churches (based upon 2 Thessalonians 2:2, 3:17) that eventually made its way into the hands of the church members at Thessalonica. The letter appeared to have come from Paul which caused confusion. Whether this is true or not, the Thessalonians worried they had somehow missed the Lord's return, and the present lawlessness they were witnessing seemed to confirm their fear. The enemy was at work within the young church. The truth was being twisted and the Thessalonians were doubting what they knew. Trying to alleviate their fears and desiring for their hearts to trust God again, Paul wrote to them. In his letter, he set the record straight about what they should anticipate and exhorted them on how they should live as they waited and endured the evil around them. Paul desired that they would stand fast while holding tightly to what they knew to be true and not be shaken with fear.

> PAUL DESIRED THAT THEY WOULD STAND FAST WHILE HOLDING TIGHTLY TO WHAT THEY KNEW TO BE TRUE AND NOT BE SHAKEN WITH FEAR.

In Matthew 11 Jesus highlighted the ministry of a man who stood firmly on the truth and fearlessly rebuked sin; that man was John the Baptist. When speaking to the multitudes, Jesus asked them, "What did you go out into the wilderness to see? A reed shaken by the wind?" Those in the audience knew John was no trembling reed who was easily swayed by his circumstances or prevailing popular opinion. He had remained steadfast as a rock while rebuking sin and pointing out their cultural moral decline. He would not be swayed because his roots ran deep and were planted firmly upon the coming Messiah.

Paul desired the Thessalonians to have the kind of steadfastness Jesus pointed out in John the Baptist. He desired and expressed in 2 Thessalonians 2 that they would "not be soon shaken in mind or troubled in spirit" and reminded them to "stand fast and hold to the traditions" they were taught. God loved the Thessalonians and would one day reunite them unto Himself. They did not have to worry or be afraid because their salvation was secure. They could rest in the knowledge of this truth and be at peace in troubled times. We can, too, if we take the words of 2 Thessalonians 2 to heart knowing that God knows and sees all. He has a timetable and a plan which will come to pass. We can stand firm and not be shaken like a reed in the wind even though things around us are constantly in flux. We have a sure foundation because "God our Father, who has loved us and given us everlasting consolation and good hope by grace" will comfort our hearts and will firmly keep us until the day we see Him face to face.

Open in Prayer

Prepare your heart before studying by filling in the prayer prompts and praying them back to the Lord as you begin.

God, You are…

God, forgive me for…

God, thank You for…

God, please help me…

Receiving God's Word

Read 2 Thessalonians 2

Experiencing God's Word

| Paul addresses the fears and concerns regarding the Antichrist and Christ's return (2:1-12) | Paul's theological assurance of their salvation (2:13-15) | Paul's prayer for the Thessalonians to stand firm (2:16-17) |

EXPERIENCE 1 (10 minutes)

OBSERVATION OF 2 THESSALONIANS 2:1–17

Following are verse-by-verse questions to help you get a broad understanding of the chapter. The answers will be found directly in the text.

118 | CAUGHT UP

1. Read 2 Thessalonians 2:1–2. What words suggest the Thessalonians were worried and afraid and why?

2. According to verse 3, what must occur before the Day of the Lord?

3. How is the son of perdition described in verse 4?

4. Read verses 5–7. Who is restraining the lawless one right now?

5. Use verse 8 to explain what will eventually happen to the lawless one.

6. Who in verses 9–10 is working through the lawless one and is invoking fear?

7. According to verses 11–12, how does God confirm the decision of those who reject Him?

8. What does Paul say in verses 13–15 to alleviate the fears and worries of the Thessalonians?

9. How does Paul in verses 16–17 point the Thessalonians to the Lord in their fears?

> ### CONSIDER
>
> Consider how fear, worry, and deception can work together causing godly truth to be questioned as well as a falling away to result. Consider how this happens and note your thoughts below.
>
> _____
> _____
> _____
> _____

EXPERIENCE 2 (20 minutes)

WORLDLY WORRIES
2 Thessalonians 2:1–12

Fear and worry are powerful tools of the enemy. They can distract, shake our faith, and weigh us down if allowed. Worry can take our minds away from focusing on God and choosing to trust Him. Knowing the fear and the power it held over the Thessalonians, Paul wanted them to be free from their worries. In these verses, he turns them back to the Lord, our ultimate source of stability in troubling times.

1. Read 2 Thessalonians 2:1–2. The Thessalonians are watching things happen around them that are fear-inducing. Using verse 2, list the ways Paul notices how fear is coming upon the Thessalonians.

2. According to verse 3, what is the root of the Thessalonian's fears?

3. What did Paul say in verse 3 to combat their fears regarding the coming of the Lord?

4. Read the following verses that address the revealing of the son of perdition who is also known in Scripture as the antichrist, the lawless one, and the beast. Note what you learn about how he will reveal himself.

   - Matthew 24:15

   - Daniel 9:27 & 11:36
     (Note in Daniel 9 that one week equals 7 years of tribulation, so the middle of the tribulation will be after 3.5 years)

   - Revelation 13:1, 6–8

   - 2 Corinthians 11:14

5. Verse 4 describes the antichrist, and verse 9 tells us that the antichrist works under Satan's power. Read Isaiah 14:13–14. These verses describe the fall of Satan (who once was an angel of God named Lucifer). What do you see in Isaiah 14 that parallels 2 Thessalonians 2:4 regarding the character of the antichrist and his intentions?

DEEPER EXPERIENCE

"The man of sin is truly an Anti-Christ. Satan has planned the career of the man of sin to mirror the ministry of Jesus.

- Both Jesus and the man of sin have a coming (2 Thessalonians 2:1 and 2:9).
- Both Jesus and the man of sin are revealed (2 Thessalonians 1:7 and 2:3).
- Both Jesus and the man of sin have a gospel (2 Thessalonians 2:10–11).
- Both Jesus and the man of sin say that they alone should be worshiped (2 Thessalonians 2:4).
- Both Jesus and the man of sin have support for their claims by miraculous works (2 Thessalonians 2:9).

"Clearly, the man of sin is Satan's parody of the true Messiah…The coming of Jesus and the judgment of God will make it clear that the man of sin is not God at all." (David Guzik, www.blueletterbible.org)

6. Read 2 Thessalonians 2:5–7. Paul reminded them of his previous teachings and the great falling away from God. Paul distinguishes between the coming of the antichrist and the ongoing lawlessness in the world. Read 1 John 2:18–19 and 2 John 7. How is the mystery of lawlessness already at work?

   a. According to 1 John 2:20–22, how are believers able to recognize his deception?

DEEPER EXPERIENCE

"Before he [the antichrist] is revealed openly, the lawlessness he personifies is operating secretly. His antisocial, anti-law, anti-God movement is at present largely underground. We detect its subversive influence around us today—in the atheistic stance of secular humanism, in the totalitarian tendencies of extreme left-wing and right-wing ideologies, in the materialism of the consumer society which puts things in the place of God, in those so-called 'theologies' which proclaim the death of God and the end of moral absolutes, and in the social permissiveness which cheapens the sanctity of human life, sex, marriage and family, all of which God created and instituted." (John R. W. Stott, The Message of 1 & 2 Thessalonians, p. 141)

7. Read Ephesians 6:10–13. How do we combat the enemy's fearful tactics?

8. How do you see God's sovereignty in 2 Thessalonians 2:6–8?

DEEPER EXPERIENCE

> "Something or Someone is holding back the culmination of lawlessness. Part of the purpose of this restraint is to keep the man of sin from being revealed prematurely. The Holy Spirit of God is the only Person with sufficient (supernatural) power to do this restraining." (John Walvoord and Roy Zuck, The Bible Knowledge Commentary, p. 718–719)

9. According to verses 9–10, how does Satan use the lawless one to stir up fear?

10. John Stott wrote, "Behind the great deception there lay the great refusal." Use verses 10–11 to describe the slippery slope of deception and refusal.

11. Read 2 Thessalonians 2:10–12 and Romans 1:24–25. How does God confirm the decisions of the people described in 2 Thessalonians 2:1–12?

DEEPER EXPERIENCE

> *"That men will be condemned for not believing the truth, and that it will be right thus to condemn them, is everywhere the doctrine of the Scriptures, and is equally the doctrine of common sense. 'But had pleasure in unrighteousness.' This is the second ground or reason for their condemnation. If men have pleasure in sin, it is proper that they should be punished. There can be no more just ground of condemnation than that a man loves to do wrong."* (Albert Barnes, *Barnes' Notes on the New Testament: Ephesians to Philemon*, p. 92)

CONSIDER

Consider and comment how the enemy's tactics, including fear and worry, were used against the Thessalonians' faith in their present circumstances as well as their future with Christ.

_____
_____
_____
_____

EXPERIENCE 3 (20 minutes)

CHRIST'S COMFORT
2 Thessalonians 2:13–17

Once again Paul is encouraging and reassuring the Thessalonians because the enemy was deceiving many. He is relentless. Paul recognized the Thessalonians were growing weary and needed God's comfort. He brought God's consolation in words, in prayer, and in truth which ultimately pointed them back to Christ, our great Comforter. Paul speaks words of life into the lives of the young followers of Christ, reminding them to stand firm in the Lord and to hold fast to the gospel.

1. Read 2 Thessalonians 2:13–14 and Ephesians 1:4–6. Describe God's love as seen in these verses and explain why this would be a source of encouragement amid the Thessalonians' fear and worry.

a. Read 2 Timothy 1:7 and 1 John 4:18. What do you learn about fear and God's love for His people?

2. In 2 Thessalonians 2:10–12 God confirms the unbelievers in their rejection of Him. Go back and look at your answers to question 10 of Experience 2 which looked at these verses. Compare and contrast the unbeliever's rejection in verses 2:10–12 with the believer's acceptance described in verse 2:13. Write your answers below.

- Rejected:

- Accepted:

b. What was Paul's purpose for reminding them of their decision? Why do believers need this kind of reminder, especially when fear is present?

3. Read 2 Thessalonians 2:14. How does God call people to Himself and for what ultimate purpose?

a. Use verse 14 to explain the importance of evangelism.

4. To give further understanding to 2 Thessalonians 2:14, read John 17:22–23 and 1 Peter 5:1. How do God's calling and glory fit together in the life of the believer?

DEEPER EXPERIENCE

> "The biblical doctrine of divine election has always perplexed Christian people. Yet, although it perplexes our minds, it greatly comforts our hearts, and it is entirely consistent with our experience. We know the truth of Jesus' words, 'You did not choose Me, but I chose you.' For we remember, before God laid hold of us, how stubborn, rebellious, and weak we were. There is, therefore, no option but to trace our salvation back beyond our 'decision' or 'commitment' (i.e., conversion) to the gracious initiative of God, and say 'God chose us…. God called us.'" (John R. W. Stott, The Message of 1 & 2 Thessalonians, p. 145)

5. Paul starts 2 Thessalonians 2:15 with the word, "therefore," tying the previous verses to what he is now saying. He then gives two commands. Despite the unstable circumstances they faced, what are the Thessalonians commanded to do as they live among evil and deception? Knowing the assurances Paul gave them, what could have been the temptation for the Thessalonians?

6. What does it mean in verse 15 to stand firm and hold fast?

DEEPER EXPERIENCE

> *"The noun here rendered 'teachings' (paradoseis), consistently rendered 'traditions' in the KJV, literally means 'the things handed on' and denotes the teachings passed on from teacher to pupil. The term was a part of the early church vocabulary relating to the transmission of the gospel message. 'This tradition terminology,' Moore remarks, 'will have been adopted into the Christian vocabulary from Jewish custom and usage, for Jews were used to thinking of their law as delivered by God to Moses who in turn delivered it to Joshua, and so on.' " (D. Edmond Hiebert, 1 & 2 Thessalonians, p. 354)*

7. Read 2 Thessalonians 2:16–17. Paul ends this chapter with a prayer for the Thessalonians. Based on his prayer, how is God ultimately the source of all comfort?

CONSIDER

Consider how Paul hinges everything, both now and in the future, around the love (2:13, 2:16) of Jesus Christ. How does the love of Christ bring stability and assurance when worldly worries are present?

_____
_____
_____
_____

ACTING ON GOD'S WORD

The words *fear not* are used 63 times in the King James version of the Bible. Fear and worry are referenced nearly 500 times. Clearly, God knew we would be prone to fear and anxiety in unstable circumstances. Knowing this, He gave us instructions on how to counter Satan's spiritual attacks on our faith. Whereas Paul did not use the words fear and worry directly in 2 Thessalonians 2, he did identify the product of fear and worry in the lives of the young believers. They were shaken in mind and troubled in spirit (2 Thess. 2:2) regarding the evil surrounding them. Not wanting the Thessalonians to get caught up in their emotions and stop trusting God, he encouraged them in the Lord. He dispelled the evil one and reminded them of their spiritual foundation in Christ.

The sinful, human heart hasn't changed in 2,000 years, neither has the enemy's ways. Just as the Thessalonians encountered evil, uncertainty, lawlessness, and attacks on biblical truths, so do we today. As much as the world can shout disaster, disease, financial collapse, political upheaval, and more, God whispers to our hearts, *"Fear not, for I am with you; be not dismayed, for I am your God. I will strengthen you, yes, I will help you, I will uphold you with My righteous right hand"* Isaiah 41:10.

> NOT WANTING THE THESSALONIANS TO GET CAUGHT UP IN THEIR EMOTIONS AND STOP TRUSTING GOD, HE ENCOURAGED THEM IN THE LORD.

As Paul spoke into the fears of the Thessalonians, let the Holy Spirit speak into the possible fears in your heart as you apply the lessons from our verses.

1. What areas of life have, or could potentially have, a spirit of fear or anxiety in your heart? List them below.

2. Having stability in an unstable world can only come from the Lord. One way the enemy causes fear is by creating doubt in God by deceiving us through our circumstances. Fear usually has a root of deception attached to it. Consider the fears you listed above. Ask God to show you the root cause of that fear. Is there a lie you are believing as the Thessalonians were?

3. As Paul demonstrated, truth combats doubt and deceptions. What truths about God can help you in times of fear? How have you seen the truths of God's character bring you stability?

4. Paul stated what science has since proven. Fear and worry start in the mind and show up in our actions. The Thessalonians were being shaken in their minds, so Paul exhorted them to stand firm and hold fast to the Lord. What tangible things can you do to stand strong in the Lord and hold firmly to Him as a way of helping you during times of fear/worry?

5. It is said that worry is a conversation you have with yourself about things you cannot change. Prayer is a conversation you have with God about things He can do. End by writing a prayer to God that expresses any of your fears. Model your prayer similar to the prayer Paul said for the Thessalonians in verses 16–17.

DELIGHTING IN GOD'S WORD

GET CAUGHT UP IN SCRIPTURE

Read Week 8's memory verse from the cards you cut apart from the back of your workbook. Next, write the verse below to encourage your memorization of it, and then place the card somewhere you will see it throughout the week.

2 Thessalonians 2:13

Try to memorize the verses on all eight memory cards by the time you finish the study.

Close in Prayer

WEEK 8: DON'T GET CAUGHT UP IN FEAR AND WORRY

Teaching Title _____

Teaching Videos and handouts are available for free at www.delightinginthelord.com.

WEEK 8: DON'T GET CAUGHT UP IN FEAR AND WORRY

Teaching Title _____

Teaching Videos and handouts are available for free at www.delightinginthelord.com.

WEEK 9

DON'T GET CAUGHT UP IN DISTRACTIONS

Throughout our study of 1 and 2 Thessalonians, we've learned a lot about this newly formed church in Thessalonica. Through their faith, love, and enduring hope, we've seen the evidence of Christ in their lives, even amid trials and persecutions. We've heard testimony of how their lives were a witness for Christ to those around them, both close by and far away. We've learned of some of their internal and external struggles over fear and worry concerning the Lord's return. Paul covered a lot of ground in two short letters.

These young believers seemed to be on the fast track of Christian growth. It has been noted by commentators that Paul's letters to the Thessalonians contain teachings on nearly every doctrinal truth regarding our faith in Christ. Paul carefully included every encouragement and caution they would need to successfully run their individual spiritual race.

As much as we learned about the Thessalonian believers, we also witnessed Paul's testimony lived out. From the moment he was saved, he lived his life on a mission from God, equipped by the Holy Spirit and led by God's truth. What Paul received from God, he put into action and lovingly shared. Why was he so passionate and direct? Maybe because he wanted nothing more than for the gospel to go forward unhindered. Paul personally knew the pitfalls around him and knew they were no different for the church. As Paul ran his spiritual race with diligence, determination, and conviction, he also wanted the Thessalonians to run their race well. With that in mind, the last subject he touches on is distractions. What are those things that hinder our focus, turn our gaze away from Christ, or even trip us up into areas of sin?

> WHAT ARE THOSE THINGS THAT HINDER OUR FOCUS, TURN OUR GAZE AWAY FROM CHRIST, OR EVEN TRIP US UP INTO AREAS OF SIN?

In 1 Corinthians 9, Paul compares the Christian life with a race, which he does often and can even be found in 2 Thessalonians 3. He begins by praying the word of God would run swiftly. If the word runs swiftly, it must be carried by swift runners. It's like Paul ends his letter by telling the Thessalonians to gear up again for the next leg of their God-given race toward glory. He lays out the course they need to run in light of Christ's soon-coming return. As you read these final 18 verses, listen to Paul coaching them as they run. Keep looking to Jesus! Keep running! Jump the hurdles! Run with purpose! And above all, don't get caught up in earthly distractions that will hinder your race or the spread of the gospel.

As Paul cheers on the Thessalonians, he's cheering us on too. Finally, sweet sister, stay the course! Run well! And above all, remember God is faithful and will see you through the race to the finish line!

Open in Prayer

Prepare your heart before studying by filling in the prayer prompts and praying them back to the Lord as you begin.

God, You are…

God, forgive me for…

God, thank You for…

God, please help me…

RECEIVING GOD'S WORD

Read 2 Thessalonians 3

EXPERIENCING GOD'S WORD

Prayer, evangelism, and obedience (3:1-5) → Work diligently without distraction (3:6-15) → Closing prayer (3:16-18)

EXPERIENCE 1 (10 minutes)

OBSERVATION OF 2 THESSALONIANS 3:1–18

Following are verse-by-verse questions to help you get a broad understanding of the chapter. The answers will be found directly in the text.

1. Read 2 Thessalonians 3:1–2. What personal prayer requests does Paul ask the Thessalonians to pray on behalf of himself, Silas, and Timothy?

2. List the attributes Paul ascribes to the Lord in verse 3.

3. Paul says in verse 4 that he has confidence. What is the foundation and purpose of his confidence?

4. What is required of the Thessalonians in verse 4?

5. How does Paul want the Thessalonians' hearts to be directed? What is their sustenance according to verse 5?

6. Read 2 Thessalonians 3:6. What command does Paul give the Thessalonians?

7. Read verses 7–9. What was the example set before the Thessalonians concerning their day-to-day conduct?

8. According to verses 10–11, what are the consequences for not working? Describe how the Thessalonians should live and work.

9. What does Paul call those who are lazy and idle with their time? What command does he give in verses 11–12?

10. What encouragement does Paul offer in 2 Thessalonians 3:13 to those working diligently?

11. What final set of instructions does Paul give in verses 14–15 concerning those who will not obey what Paul has commanded?

12. How is the Lord described in verse 16?

13. According to verses 17–18, how does Paul authenticate that he is the author of the letter? Look at the last sentence of the letter. What does he say is his desire for the Thessalonians?

CONSIDER

Consider Paul's final words to the Thessalonians regarding distractions. Why is Paul so concerned about the different ways believers become distracted? Consider how he includes himself in the exhortations.

_____

_____

_____

_____

EXPERIENCE 2 (20 minutes)

READY, SET…
2 Thessalonians 3:1–5

Just as a runner prepares at the starting line for a race, it is as if the Thessalonians are kneeling at the starting block preparing to run a deeper race of faith. Distractions are everywhere and are trying to deter them from trusting God. Paul reminds them God is faithful. Stay the course.

It's as though Paul is encouraging them to brace their feet so they don't slip as they wait for the sound of the starter's pistol in the spiritual race set before them. Paul asks the Thessalonians to pray for him and to understand their purpose before the Lord as a co-laborer. He, too, has a race that he's running alongside them. The Thessalonians have work to do to support God's commission through Paul as he shares the gospel. Paul lays out their role, and he exhorts them to run in obedience. He reminds them once again that as they trust in God, He will supply all they need.

---

1. Read 2 Thessalonians 3:1–2. Describe how Paul was a man on a mission, undeterred in direction and focus for the Lord.

a. What hindrances does Paul share regarding his mission?

b. Write adjectives describing Paul as he is seen in these verses.

c. Does Paul work in isolation? Explain why or why not based on verses 1–2.

2. Paul said in 1 Thessalonians 1:8 that the word of the Lord has "sounded forth," comparing it to a trumpet's sound. How does he speak again about the word of the Lord in verses 1–2? What is his comparison?

DEEPER EXPERIENCE

"God's Word is alive (Hebrews 4:12); we must let it move freely. Paul alluded here to Psalm 147:15—'He sendeth forth His commandment upon earth: His word runneth very swiftly.' God's servants may be bound, but God's Word cannot be bound (2 Tim. 2:9). As we practice the truth and pray for the ministry of the truth, God's Word will have freedom to run and accomplish God's purposes in the world." (Warren Wiersbe, Be Ready: Living in Light of Christ's Return, p.165)

3. Read 1 Corinthians 9:24–27. Paul often used athletic imagery in his teachings. How does Paul use this imagery for himself, the Christian, and evangelism?

4. Despite the gospel going forth in power, Paul points out a sad reality in 2 Thessalonians 3:2b. What is this sad truth? Why do you think Paul made mention of it? How can these people be a distraction?

5. A foundational truth is stated about the Lord in verse 3. What does it mean that the Lord is faithful?

6. Look up the following verses about God's faithfulness and note what you learn.

    - Psalm 91:4–6

    - 1 Corinthians 10:13

    - 1 Thessalonians 5:23–24

7. Define the word *establish* either in your own words or with the help of a dictionary.

    a. Use verse 3 to explain why the Thessalonians need to be established and guarded. How does God's faithfulness impact this need?

WEEK 9: DON'T GET CAUGHT UP IN DISTRACTIONS | 139

8. Read 1 Corinthians 1:4–9. How does Paul's message to the Corinthians give further understanding of what Paul is saying to the Thessalonians in verse 4? How is Paul's confidence ultimately in the Lord concerning the Thessalonians? Explain for what purpose.

   a. How can confidence be misplaced when it comes to the Christian walk and evangelism?

9. Read 1 Corinthians 13:1–3. How do these verses help explain why Paul desires God to direct the Thessalonians' hearts in agape love and steadfast endurance as seen in 2 Thessalonians 3:5?

10. Go back to 1 Thessalonians 1:2–5 and compare how Paul opened his first letter to the Thessalonians with his thoughts as he ends his last letter in 2 Thessalonians 3:1–5. What similarities are seen? What conclusions can you draw from the similarities?

CONSIDER

Prayer has been a central focus for Paul throughout his letters to the Thessalonians. Consider and comment on the subjects, recipients, and intercessors Paul has addressed and why.

_____
_____
_____
_____

EXPERIENCE 3 (20 minutes)

GO!
2 Thessalonians 3:6–18

At this point in the letter, it is as if the starter's pistol has sounded, and the Thessalonians are off and running. Paul, much like a concerned coach, gives additional instruction as he runs beside them. He encourages them to run without hindrances and to focus on what is important. He reminds them of how he lived his life as an example for them to follow. He warns them about the pitfalls of allowing others' idleness to rub off on them and then closes the letter with a loving prayer.

1. Paul commands the Thessalonians to withdraw from certain people. How does Paul describe these people in 2 Thessalonians 3:6, 11, and 15?

    a. Withdrawal is different from sending someone away. Why should they separate from these people?

2. Paul was very careful to maintain a good testimony for the Lord. Through his example, and that of Silas and Timothy, Paul contrasted a disorderly life with one of godly order in verses 7–9. How is work tied to a good testimony in these verses?

3. God-ordained work goes all the way back to the creation of mankind. Read Genesis 2:15 and 3:17–19 & 23. Describe God's call to work before and after sin entered the heart of mankind. What change occurred and why?

4. The Bible is full of examples of those who worked. Read the following verses and give the name of the person as well as their job.

    - Genesis 6:13–14

    - 1 Samuel 17:34–35

    - Matthew 13:55

    - Acts 18:3

5. Read 2 Thessalonians 3:10 and 1 Timothy 5:8. What do these verses say about those who refuse to work?

6. In 1 Thessalonians 4:11 Paul warned the Thessalonians in a way that was like his warning in 2 Thessalonians 3:11. Based on these verses, how can idleness lead to being a busybody?

7. Idleness is a breeding ground for sin. What does Paul suggest in 2 Thessalonians 3:12 as a remedy for a busybody?

8. Read 2 Thessalonians 3:13. In your own words describe why this verse would encourage the weary Thessalonian believers who were witnessing busybodies not working as they should.

DEEPER EXPERIENCE

"Do not grow weary in doing good: This was a proper encouragement for those who were working as they should. Few things are more wearying than seeing others take advantage of Christian generosity. But we should never let the manipulations of some discourage us from doing good to the truly needy." (David Guzik, www.blueletterbible.org)

9. Paul has often alluded to the idea that the Thessalonians were a family. Read 2 Thessalonians 3:14–15. When members of a family are distracted and unwilling to work, they should receive instruction and then discipline as needed. Describe the discipline Paul recommends toward a brother in the faith who does not obey his instruction. What message does this discipline communicate to those both inside the church (believers) and outside the church (unbelievers)?

   a. Is Paul suggesting that the body of Christ shouldn't help those in the body of Christ struggling financially or struggling to find employment? Explain.

WEEK 9: DON'T GET CAUGHT UP IN DISTRACTIONS | 143

10. Read 2 Thessalonians 3:16–18. How does Paul's prayer for peace seem particularly important considering what he just taught in verses 6–15? How might peace be lacking among them?

   a. Why would seeing Paul's signature at the end of the letter encourage peace regarding the instruction contained within the letter?

   b. Why would grace be one of the most important qualities that covers all the instructions Paul gave in the letter?

> ### CONSIDER
>
> Consider the specific distractions that Paul warned of in this chapter. Distractions were coming from outside the church and within the church. Consider the remedy Paul has given for all the distractions that come upon us as we try to live for Christ, whether they are inside the church or outside. Comment below.
>
> _____
>
> _____
>
> _____
>
> _____

Acting on God's Word

Many of us are likely familiar with the term writer's block, but unless you are a runner, you may not be familiar with the term runner's block. Runner's block can occur when you feel too tired or too busy to run. It can begin in your mind but can also occur after an injury. No matter how it develops, runner's block can hinder forward progress and, in some cases, stop a person from running altogether.

Hebrews 12:1–3 compares living the Christian life to a race. We are called to throw off anything that hinders or entangles us from running with perseverance and joy. We are told to fix our eyes on Jesus and run the race as He did by enduring difficulty with the end of the race in mind.

> WE ARE CALLED TO THROW OFF ANYTHING THAT HINDERS OR ENTANGLES US FROM RUNNING WITH PERSEVERANCE AND JOY.

For most of us who have put our trust in Christ, this is our daily desire. We want to be undistracted runners who are joyfully running our race; however, if we are honest, we know that this is not always our day-to-day reality. And because the Christian life isn't typically a quick sprint, but rather a marathon, we can find ourselves having a hard time as the race wears on mile after mile. Distractions are everywhere as we run our course. Let's consider how a believer can avoid runner's block, stay focused, and finish the race well.

1. Put a checkmark next to anything in this list (or write your own) that you find is a distraction from running the Christian race well.

    _____ Social media

    _____ Streaming TV series

    _____ Materialistic desires

    _____ Relationships

    _____ Productivity (To-do list)

    _____ Hobbies

    _____ Other: _____

2. Do you find that staying focused and being undistracted is easier, harder, or the same as it was for you 5, 10, or even 15+ years ago? What has changed to cause it to be easier or harder?

3. Paul encouraged the Thessalonians to stay in the race by praying (3:1), trusting God against the evil one (3:3), obedience (3:4), loving one another (3:5), avoiding idleness (3:11), and not growing weary in doing good (3:13). Describe how you can employ one of these encouragements to combat the distraction you identified.

4. Paul addressed idleness as a distraction, but busyness can sometimes be just as much of a distraction. How have you seen both idleness and busyness as distractions in your life? How are they springboards for sinful behaviors?

5. We have reached the end of our study on 1 & 2 Thessalonians. As you think back over the study, what was…

- Encouraging to you?

- Convicting to you?

- Your favorite verse?

- A meaningful action you took toward change?

- Something you learned more about?

- Something you will be praying about?

DELIGHTING IN GOD'S WORD

GET CAUGHT UP IN SCRIPTURE

Read Week 9's memory verse from the cards you cut apart from the back of your workbook. Next, write the verse below to encourage your memorization of it, and then place the card somewhere you will see it throughout the week.

2 Thessalonians 3:13

Commit 2 Thessalonians 3:13 to memory. Review all the verses you memorized throughout the study.

Close in Prayer

WEEK 9: DON'T GET CAUGHT UP IN DISTRACTIONS

Teaching Title _____

Teaching Videos and handouts are available for free at www.delightinginthelord.com.

WEEK 9: DON'T GET CAUGHT UP IN DISTRACTIONS

Teaching Title _____

Teaching Videos and handouts are available for free at www.delightinginthelord.com.

SCRIPTURE MEMORY CARDS

Week 2
CAUGHT UP IN THE GOSPEL

"For our gospel did not come to you in word only, but also in power, and in the Holy Spirit and in much assurance, as you know what kind of men we were among you for your sake."

1 Thessalonians 1:5

Week 3
CAUGHT UP IN PLEASING GOD

"But as we have been approved by God to be entrusted with the gospel, even so we speak, not as pleasing men, but God who tests our hearts."

1 Thessalonians 2:4

Week 4
CAUGHT UP IN A FAITH-FILLED LIFE

"And may the Lord make you increase and abound in love to one another and to all, just as we do to you, so that He may establish your hearts blameless in holiness before our God and Father at the coming of our Lord Jesus Christ with all His saints."

1 Thessalonians 3:12-13

Week 5
CAUGHT UP WITH AN ETERNAL PERSPECTIVE

"For the Lord Himself will descend from heaven with a shout, with the voice of an archangel, with the trumpet of God. And the dead in Christ will rise first. Then we who are alive and remain shall be caught up together with them in the clouds to meet the Lord in the air. And thus we shall always be with the Lord."

1 Thessalonians 4:16-17

Week 6
CAUGHT UP IN GOD'S WILL

"Now may the God of peace Himself sanctify you completely; and may your whole spirit, soul and body be preserved blameless at the coming of our Lord Jesus Christ. He who calls you is faithful, who also will do it."

1 Thessalonians 5:23-24

Week 7
DON'T GET CAUGHT UP IN YOUR CIRCUMSTANCES

"Therefore, we also pray always for you that our God would count you worthy of this calling, and fulfill all the good pleasure of His goodness and the work of faith with power."

2 Thessalonians 1:11

Week 8
DON'T GET CAUGHT UP IN FEAR AND WORRY

"But we are bound to give thanks to God always for you, brethren beloved by the Lord, because God from the beginning chose you for salvation through sanctification by the Spirit and belief in the truth."

2 Thessalonians 2:13

Week 9
DON'T GET CAUGHT UP IN DISTRACTIONS

"But as for you, brethren, do not grow weary in doing good."

2 Thessalonians 3:13

Page intentionally left blank / back side of Memory Cards

WORKS CITED

Barnes, Albert. *Barnes' Notes on the New Testament: Ephesians to Philemon*. Baker Book House Company, 2005.

CLC International. *CLC Bible Companion*. Christian Literature Crusade, 2011.

Hiebert, D. Edmond. *1 & 2 Thessalonians*. BMH Books, 1992.

Ironside, H.A. *1 & 2 Thessalonians: Ironside Commentaries*. Loizeaux Brothers, Inc., 1997.

Nelson's NKJV Study Bible. Thomas Nelson, Inc., 1997.

Phillips, John. *Exploring 1 & 2 Thessalonians: An Expository Commentary*. Kregel Publications, 2005.

Stott, John R. W. *1 & 2 Thessalonians: Living in the End Times*. Intervarsity Press, 1998.

Stott, John R. W. *The Message of 1 & 2 Thessalonians*. Intervarsity Press, 1991 (Revised 2021).

Walvoord, John F., and Roy B. Zuck. *The Bible Knowledge Commentary: An Exposition of the Scriptures by Dallas Seminary Faculty: New Testament*. Victor Books, 1985.

Wiersbe, Warren W. *Be Ready: Living in Light of Christ's Return: NT Commentary, 1 & 2 Thessalonians*. David C. Cook, 2010.

Wiersbe, Warren W. *The Bible Exposition Commentary*. Victor Books, 1989.

www.bible.org

www.blueletterbible.org

www.jesuswalk.com/thessalonians/00_intro.htm(map of Thessalonians)

www.merriam-webster.com/dictionary/ballast

OTHER DELIGHTING IN THE LORD STUDIES

Being An Everyday Esther
A Study on the Book of Esther (Amazon)
9-Week Study

A Jewish girl, orphaned at a young age, living in a foreign land, and raised by her cousin...her story starts as one of uncertain circumstances and hopeless situations. And yet, Esther doesn't let her circumstances define her or hold her back from being used by God to save the Jewish nation from certain destruction. Esther is a woman of God whose life is defined by the one true sovereign God of the Israelites.

God will open doors for Esther to gain a position of influence and prominence in Persia as she goes from orphan to queen. It was "for such a time as this" that God would call upon Esther's faith to act in courage and help save the Jewish people from genocide under the hand of an evil Persian leader. The book of Esther is a story of rags to riches, life or death moments, and faith triumphing over fear. Esther's life is a testimony for all of us of God's love, as well as an example of what it looks like to be a devoted woman of God.

A Fresh Start
A Study on the Book of Ezra (Amazon)
9-Week Study

Who doesn't love a fresh start?
Within the pages of Ezra is a story of God's faithfulness to His people who were given a fresh start after ongoing disobedience to His commands. For 70 years in Babylonian captivity, God, desiring for them to turn back to Him, lovingly and mercifully dealt with their sinful hearts and then led them back to Jerusalem.

You will be inspired to put the past behind you and begin again as you learn more about God who restores, rebuilds, and revives His people.

OTHER DELIGHTING IN THE LORD STUDIES

Know Him: Light, Love, Truth
A Study on the Books of 1,2,3 John (Amazon)
9-Week Study

We live in a world characterized by false information. The truth about Jesus Christ, salvation in Him, and eternity with Him has become clouded with misunderstanding. The study of 1,2,3 John will clearly explain, through John's firsthand experience, who Jesus Christ is and the importance of knowing Him who is light, love and truth.

A Proven, Active, Faithful Walk
A Study on the Book of James (Amazon)
9-Week Study

What does your life say about your faith in Jesus? That is the question James will drive home. In five short-but-mighty chapters, James will speak to each of us about how our lives prove our faith. Leaving few areas of our lives unexamined, James stresses a true saving faith will reveal itself in a proven, active, faithful walk with Christ.

Delighting In Christ: Rooted, Built Up, and Established
A Study on the Book of Colossians (Amazon)
9-Week Study

This study addresses Christ's preeminence over all areas of the believer's life. Paul warns the church at Colossae to beware of false teachings by reinforcing the truth of Jesus Christ. The study encourages those who follow Jesus to be rooted, built up, and established in Him.

OTHER DELIGHTING IN THE LORD STUDIES

Delighting in the King of Kings: Matthew Volume 1: Chapters 1–9 (Amazon) 9 Weeks
Delighting in the King of Kings: Matthew Volume 2: Chapters 10–20 (Amazon) 11 Weeks
Delighting in the King of Kings: Matthew Volume 3: Chapters 21–28 (Amazon) 8 Weeks
28-Week Study Total

Study the life of the King of Kings, Jesus Christ, from His birth to His ascension from the perspective of the gospel writer Matthew. This series is written as a three-volume set but can be studied individually.

Delighting in God's Wisdom: Proverbs (Amazon)
13-Week Study

Gain wisdom from the book of Proverbs while learning from examples of women in the Bible. King Solomon is the primary writer of this book and sets forth insights on how to solve many of life's challenges.

Delighting in a Life of Triumph:
A Study on the Life of Joseph from Genesis 37–50
(Amazon) 9-Week Study

Examine what triumphant living can look like, even when faced with challenging family relationships, being wrongly accused, and forgotten by those who should have loved you. The life of Joseph is a powerful testimony about how to live victoriously amidst life's difficult circumstances.

OTHER DELIGHTING IN THE LORD STUDIES

Delighting in a Life Lived for God: A Study on the Book of 1 Peter
(Amazon)
10-Week Study

Study the encouragement given by the disciple Peter on how to live a perfected, established, strengthened, and settled life in the Lord while in the midst of difficulty, trials, and persecution.

Additional verse-by-verse studies can be found at www.delightinginthelord.com.
These studies were used in the women's ministry at Calvary Chapel Chester Springs.
Any study can be downloaded for free from the Delighting in the Lord ministry website.
Each study has video teachings that accompany the weekly lessons.

The studies are:

Delighting in the Holy Spirit: Acts
26-Week Study

Delighting in God's Heart: The Life of David through 1 & 2 Samuel and the Psalms
24-Week Study

Delighting in the Redeemer: A Love Story from the book of Ruth
4-Week Study

Delighting in God's Will and His Provision: Jonah & Nahum
7-Week Study

Delighting in God, His Righteousness, and Perfect Plan: Romans
17-Week Study

< Scan this code with your phone to find out more about Delighting In the Lord.

www.delightinginthelord.com

< Scan this code with your phone to access the free downloads for all bible studies as well as view the teaching videos that accompany each Bible study.

www.cc-chestersprings.com/resources/ditl-series/

For weekly encouragement and updates on the ministry, please follow us on social media.
Facebook: Delighting in the Lord Ministry • Instagram: ditl_ministry

Made in the USA
Columbia, SC
27 January 2025